Wow. I've never read a book like this one before! Who would ever guess that a few reflections on wind and waves, shipwrecks and sea monsters, could comfort and challenge so profoundly? Jonathan Martin writes with a pastor's heart and poet's touch, taking the reader to colorful, unexpected places with each turn of the page. His insights into Scripture are fresh, his storytelling honest and vulnerable. *How to Survive a Shipwreck* is a book to be savored, cherished, and returned to. I suspect it will take its place among some of the finest spiritual memoirs of our time.

> **Rachel Held Evans,** bestselling author of *Searching for Sunday* and *A Year of Biblical Womanhood*

Be warned: Jonathan Martin's title is a bit misleading. What he has packaged as a sort of shipwreck "survival kit" turns out to be a force of prose by which we are swept to the shore of Malta with a raging velocity that is at once raw and redemptive. Also we are urged to eat cheesecake tonight, for our own good. I love this book.

> **Steven Furtick,** lead pastor of Elevation Church, Charlotte, North Carolina, and author of *Crash the Chatterbox*

If Southern gothic theology was a genre of writing, this may be our generation's undomesticated, spirit-haunted introduction. Poet-prophet-preacher Jonathan Martin has come to us speaking in tongues of fire as a howl and a song from the sea, from life after everything is lost. This gorgeous book is deep water, terrible and beautiful and cleansing; the words smell of salt water and wine, bread and longing, grief and hope. All of us who have on̶ gone under will weep with aching recogni̶ tifies to the loving God who meets u̶ and monsters to set us utterly free thr̶ look at all like we thought it would.

> **Sarah Bessey,** author of *J̶ ̶ ̶ ̶* and *Out of Sorts: Making Peace with an Evolving Faith*

Gritty and transcendent. *How to Survive a Shipwreck* isn't really any kind of how-to book. Rather, Jonathan Martin takes us on a stunning and stark voyage of his own soul's deep dive and near drowning. You won't reach for any well-fixed, handy life preservers here—Martin doesn't throw us any. There are plenty of "storm" books out there, swollen with platitudes and simple strategies for recovery. These pages are dripping instead with ache and beauty. A harrowing hope. His writing is mesmeric and will fill your lungs enough to ascend and take that first big breath at the water's surface. The breath you thought you might never take again.

Nichole Nordeman, songwriting and recording artist

Anyone who has experienced deep and transformative brokenness will resonate with this book. I did. As Jonathan Martin turned the pain of his interior death into the poetry of resurrection, I found myself saying again and again, "Yes, that's what I found to be true." Our childhood understanding of life and faith must give way to a more nuanced view of ourselves, of others, and of God. Our hearts must be broken so they can be remade. We must journey past the illusions of our own adequacy so we can discover the most important truth of all—that at the center of everything is a great Heart of love beating for us. I love this book!

Lynne Hybels, advocate for global engagement,
Willow Creek Community Church

While many people in the Western Protestant church preach a gospel that is too saccharine and simple, Jonathan Martin writes as a Christian who has experienced some real pain and loss, and the gospel that emerges from his writing is more robust and full-bodied as a result—a gospel that embraces even pain as a grace. This will be an important book for a lot of people.

Michael Gungor, singer/songwriter, coleader of the
musical collective Gungor, and member of The Liturgists

No one is more qualified to talk about the forgotten path of spiritual descent than Jonathan Martin. *How to Survive a Shipwreck* is a breakthrough in the way we are to understand our own spiritual process and conversion. His honesty and unique voice—which has been drenched in heartache, wrestling, and triumph—has deeply resonated in my life and the lives of countless others. Like so many of us, I was taught to act saved but not how to truly be born again. I believe this book is part of the antidote to help heal the great sickness of "spiritual certainty" in our world today.

William Matthews, songwriter and recording artist

Jonathan Martin is that rare soul who's been through the fire and has more, not less, hope because of it. Is he a poet or mystic or teacher or recovery expert—who cares? He has something to say.

Rob Bell, author of *How to Be Here Now* and *What We Talk about When We Talk about God*

Bob Dylan said, "Behind every beautiful thing there's been some kind of pain." I believe that's true. It's certainly true of Jonathan Martin's *How to Survive a Shipwreck.* From his bitter experience of nearly drowning in a sea of pain, Jonathan has survived to paint a beautiful portrait of a grace that will not quit. He artfully reminds us that even when we feel we are swallowed in a sea of pain, we are still enveloped in the boundless ocean of God's relentless love. This book will help and heal many shipwrecked souls.

Brian Zahnd, pastor of Word of Life Church, Saint Joseph, Missouri, and author of *Water to Wine*

Brilliant and demanding, *How to Survive a Shipwreck* is Jonathan's heart-wrenching comeback story—and it is a hidden parable for us. Can I accept one who is fallen? We are all shipwrecked. We stand in need of grace.

Dr. John Sowers, author of *The Heroic Path*

This is a stormy book—dark, fierce, jolting. And really it is not about survival but about suffering and death—and just so about resurrection and the life of faith. Over and over from beginning to end, Jonathan Martin does all he can to remind us of the gospel's deepest promise: our only hope is in letting ourselves be wrecked so we can sink into the depths of God's unrelenting devotion to our good.

Dr. Chris Green, professor of theology at Pentecost Theological Seminary and author of *Foretasting the Kingdom*

This is no preacher's sermon. This book is a survivor's confession: even while your life is violently torn apart—your heart, it can break open. Break open to a beauty, compassion, and calling you thought would never again return. Break open to a grace more powerful than the waves of pain, disaster, failure, and devastation that could so easily devour you. If you need more than self-help soothsayers and positive-thinking profiteers, Jonathan Martin invites you to undergo a baptism in grace that is deeper than the seas that would drown you.

Jarrod McKenna, Australian peace award winning pastor, activist, and cofounder of First Home Project

In this beautifully written, ruthlessly honest, often humorous, and sometimes heart-wrenching work, Jonathan Martin takes readers on a tour that intimately explores the scary, painful, dark contours of his own shipwreck. This raw but hope-filled tour leaves readers with a wealth of biblical insight on how to survive and even be transformed by the stormy times that decimate the ships of our lives.

Dr. Greg Boyd, senior pastor of Woodland Hills Church and author of twenty books, including *The Myth of a Christian Nation*

How to SURVIVE a SHIPWRECK

SHIPWRECK

Help Is on the Way
and Love Is Already Here

JONATHAN MARTIN

ZONDERVAN

How to Survive a Shipwreck
Copyright © 2016 by Jonathan Martin

Requests for information should be addressed to:
Zondervan, 3900 *Sparks Dr. SE, Grand Rapids, Michigan* 49546

ISBN 978-0-310-34798-9 (ebook)

Library of Congress Cataloging-in-Publication Data

Names: Martin, Jonathan, 1978- author.
Title: How to survive a shipwreck : help is on the way and love is already here /
    Jonathan Martin.
Description: Grand Rapids: Zondervan, 2016.
Identifiers: LCCN 2016006359 | ISBN 9780310347972 (softcover)
Subjects: LCSH: Consolation.
Classification: LCC BV4905.3 .M333 2016 | DCC 248.8/6—dc23 LC record
    available at http://lcnn.loc.gov/2016006359

Published in association with the literary agency of D. C. Jacobson and Associates LLC, an Author Management Company. www.dcjacobson.com.

Cover design: Curt Diepenhorst
Cover photography: Shutterstock
Interior design: Kait Lamphere

First Printing April 2016 / Printed in the United States of America

For everyone lost at sea,
barely holding on—
in hopes that you will yet find yourself
somehow strangely held

Deep calls to deep at the roar of your waterfalls;
    all your breakers and your waves have gone
        over me.

Psalm 42.7, ESV

the tempest
the darkness
the waves that you sent
just the saltwater taste
of these songs of descent

still sinking
still losing
the waves won't relent
I won't go down quiet
this is a song of dissent.

no flailing
no swimming
I'm not innocent
water fills my lungs
This is my song of descent.

Contents

Foreword

One thing you must know about me at the outset: I'm a sailor. My grandfathers were both sailors—both Navy men who owned sailboats in the same little harbor. My dad is a sailor. My brother sailed around the world. Our family vacations were most often spent on boats. All that to say, life on the water is deep in my bones, deep in my identity, deep in my instincts and impulses.

And one thing about sailors? We do not take the concept of shipwreck lightly. It's not an abstract idea, but an actual possibility every time you throw off the lines and leave the harbor. Every sailor knows other sailors whose boats have been struck by lightning, thrown up on rocks, tossed in heavy seas, and have had masts broken, sails torn. We don't joke about shipwrecks.

Sailors have a reputation for being foulmouthed hot dogs, rebels, devil-may-care risk takers. But in my experience, that's only partially true. They are profoundly foulmouthed—especially during races—but they are also among the most cautious people I know. Because every sailor knows how quickly and easily a shipwreck can happen.

And so when our dear friend Jonathan Martin talked with me about his book while we stood in our kitchen after church one Sunday night, I connected immediately. I understand shipwreck, both as a sailor and as a person of faith. And both as a sailor and a person of faith, I respect shipwrecks—on the water and in our souls.

It's easy to believe the goal of life is to escape unscathed—without failure, pain, or wreckage. And it's easy for Christians to believe the goal of spiritual life is to skate through with a perfect report card—no major errors or screwups.

But here's the thing: If you spend enough time on the water, something will go wrong. And if you live long enough on this beautiful, broken planet, despite your best efforts to avoid pain and check all the right boxes, things will likely fall apart at some point.

Cars will crash; marriages will explode; hearts will break. And to believe you will escape some kind of shipwreck is, at best, naive.

Shipwrecks are serious, and they're going to happen to most of us at some point. This is what we know.

What is immensely important, then, is what we do after the wreckage. I mostly know about this from doing it very, very poorly. We all have different learning styles, and mine, apparently, is making massive, painful mistakes and then writing about them in the hopes that other people can avoid them.

What I did during my first shipwreck: cling to the mast and pretend that with the force of my will, the ship would not go down. It was denial.

Another time, another shipwreck: I blamed everyone

within striking distance, and it took me months to realize I might have played a teeny-tiny part in all of it.

Yet another time: I allowed my relationship with God to become distant and rote, letting my anger obscure absolutely everything, even God's goodness, even his comfort, even his capacity to heal my broken heart.

This book is a navigational chart to guide us through the aftermath—and I could have used it during any number of storms. Because what Jonathan did after his ship was wrecked is immensely inspiring and, frankly, the opposite of what most of us do in pain and chaos.

Jonathan looked the wreckage full in the face. He peered deeply into both the lightness and the darkness of his own heart. And he drew closer to God in the middle of the mess, instead of running.

These are incredibly difficult things to do. All of our impulses urge us otherwise. But the path of growth and wholeness and love is the one that Jonathan chose, and the one that will serve as a beautiful example for so many of us as we struggle in our own storms.

This book is beautiful and deep and important, and my prayer is that it will guide you lovingly through whatever storm or shipwreck you may be facing.

Shauna Niequist,
author of *Bread and Wine*
and *Savor*

Chapter One

Losing Your Ship without Losing Your Soul

Only those who are lost will find the promised land.
Rabbi Abraham Heschel

*We are all in the same boat, in a stormy sea, and
we owe each other a terrible loyalty.*

G. K. Chesterton

The experience of drowning, through the lens of faith, is what Christians call "baptism." But no matter what you call it, the sensation of going under is entirely the same.

It was Easter Sunday at the church I founded in my hometown. I had preached on the first words of Jesus when he appeared to the disciples after his resurrection: "Do not be afraid."[1] I said you could sum up the whole of God's message to humans throughout Scripture and throughout history in those four words—*Do not be afraid.* I told our people these are words that are spoken when it would seem to us we have every reason in the world to be afraid. That

God speaks them when he is about to do something new. And in the midst of this sermon on death and resurrection, I announced I was leaving.

I felt like I was the pastor who stole Easter.

Of course, there was a part of me that felt ridiculous announcing my departure on the Sunday with the biggest attendance of the year, when everybody has dressed up and brought their friends. But I was not going to keep grabbing every rung of the ladder on the way down, trying to salvage the unsalvageable. I was not going to stay plugged into the ventilator. The only message I could preach was the only message my life could be at that point, and it was the message of death and resurrection.

Painful as it was, I knew this had to be my last sermon. I could not drag the ending out any further. I was over. I told my congregation I would be there the next Sunday for a transition service, but I would not preach again. The message of death and resurrection had finally grabbed hold of me, not in the way it grabs hold of a preacher but in the way it grabs hold of a man. I had no idea what I was walking into. I was stepping into a starless night. I only knew it was time to cash in all my chips on the hope that resurrection could be a better existence than the one I was sort of maintaining.

At the conclusion of both services, I baptized people for the last time at this church I had founded and given my life to. I felt the holiness of each of them as I gently lowered their bodies into the water, the tour guide for their own descent. I was almost done baptizing people when Heather came out of her pew with lips quivering, her face contorted in anguish. We had just buried her father, Herman, a few weeks before, and everything about his early departure was filled with ambiguity. It had been a torturous ride for her—the ordeal of her father's fall, the many hours in the hospital, the celebration that he was better and resuming normal life, the second tragic turn that led to serious decline, the weight of the decision to pull the plug.

Heather kicked off her flip-flops when she got down front and practically threw her cell phone onto the stage. As she took off her glasses and I helped her into the pool, it was not the cherubic look of a new convert on her face, excited about new faith in Jesus. It was a mix of resignation, heartbreak, an almost angry determination, and yet a kind of hope too that if she could jump into the river that carries us toward death, there could be new life for her too. Already, my nerves were jangled and my heart tender, the day being what it was. But baptizing Heather that day was something other entirely—I can't bear to not capitalize that. It was something Other.

It was my last opportunity to perform one of the sacraments I most held dear, to wash my hands in the holiness of God's sons and daughters. Heaven was skidding into the ground, and the people just kept coming and coming.

By the time I finally got done baptizing people at the second service, I looked to my right at Teddy Hart, my friend and staff pastor. He had been with me since year one, transitioning from a life of more or less biding his time in Cleveland, Tennessee, to becoming an extraordinary preacher, pastor, and friend. A sensitive soul, Teddy's eyes were already red from all the tears he had shed that morning.

"Teddy . . . do we have time for one more?"

Since it was Easter, I was wearing a suit and tie. I did not bother to change; I only took off my shoes. And I joined my people in the abyss. I loved them, and I didn't want to miss my one and only remaining opportunity to jump into the pool with them. I didn't have anybody else to baptize. My last official act as a pastor was already done. I was going to the pool, not as anybody's priest, but as one of them.

The water was cold. My heart was hot. Baptism has a celebratory aspect, but I had no delusions that those moments were anything less than my own funeral. I did not yet know what kind of man I would become when I got out of the water. I had no idea what my life would become. Like the lame man at the pool of Bethesda in the gospels, I only knew angels had been in this water, and I wanted my broken-down body in the pool, in the wake of them.

The life I had built was over. Everything I had been, I was no longer. I had no sense that the water of baptism would magic me into something more, like Clark Kent-suddenly-turned-Superman. But could the water make me, somehow, more human? I wanted to go to the pool because I wanted to embrace my full humanity in the company of my friends, vaguely aware that becoming more human is to have the image of God in us renewed.

Teddy held his hand over my nose. I felt his tears on my head. He could barely get out the words: "Pastor . . . I baptize you in the name of the Father, the Son, and the Holy

Spirit." I took the plunge. When I came up, I clutched him like a life preserver. I heard my friends weeping all around me. We all knew this was good-bye.

When There Is No Going Back to the Life You Had Before

Driven by God-knows-what kind of cocktail of nature and nurture, you build the ship you think you always wanted, board by board, or perhaps the ship someone else told you you ought to want. There's relatively little time to think about such things during the massive ego-building project that comprises much of our lives. You rarely even search your pockets anymore to try to find your misplaced reasons. Because there is another paper due, because there is another diaper to change, because there is another plane to catch, because there is another function Friday night that you simply cannot miss. And so you keep on hammering those boards, because somebody has to hammer them; you do what you do, because it's the only thing you know how to do; you keep going where you've always gone, because it's the only way you know to go.

There is nothing particularly bad about the life you've built for yourself—except you're not entirely sure if it's your life you're building, or why you're building a life at all. The world you inhabit is a long way from perfect, but it is mostly ordered. The machines are purring along; the gears are (mostly) working; the soft rhythm of established routine is just enough white noise to drown out the sound of your soul's longing, enough to help you get to sleep at night. So you can get up the next day and start it all over again, without stopping to ask why.

Until the day comes when your ship hits the rocks and you wake up to the violent sound of the sea pouring in through a hole in you. The world outside floods the insulated life you have inside, and the life you knew is now under water. Sometimes the storm crawls in slow and stealthy, catlike, until the first leak springs; sometimes the storm comes sudden, and a rushing mighty wind fills your house like some unholy ghost. It may be that the storm came outside of you and blew in the little sheet of paper on which the doctor wrote the diagnosis; or the tides dragged out the man or woman who said they'd love you forever; or you felt the air grow heavy with electric heat in the air between you on the phone when she said you lost the job. It may also well be it was you who steered straight into the rocks the ship that had kept you more or less afloat all these years—that you now hold yourself responsible for sabotaging the life you told yourself you wanted.

But it does not really matter how you got here or why; and it doesn't really matter if it was God or the devil or yourself or some ancient chaos that spilled up from the bottom of the sea. What matters now is that you are drowning, and the world you loved before is not your world any longer. The questions of why and how are less pressing than the reality that is your lungs filling with water now. Philosophy and theology won't help you much here, because what you believe existentially about storms or oceans or drowning won't make you stop drowning. Religion won't do you much good down here, because beliefs can't keep you warm when you're twenty thousand leagues beneath the sea.

There is nothing you can find in a book, including this one, that can overwhelm the hard truth you know in the five senses that will not deceive you. You see the unending blackness of a cold sea in front of you. You hear the sound of the bow—and of your own heart—snapping. You taste reality in the salt water burning in the back of your throat. You feel your blood turning to ice under the canopy of the long, arctic night.

The truth is something you already know deep in your own bones: Your ship is sinking. The life you lived before is the life you live no longer; the world you knew before is underwater now. Your life feels like a funeral, because there is a part of you that is actually dying. There are things you are losing now that you won't get back. There is a boy in you who may well be dying for you to become the man you must become now; there is a girl likely breathing her last so a more primal woman may rise to take her place.

> There is a boy in you who may well be dying for you to become the man you must become now; there is a girl likely breathing her last so a more primal woman may rise to take her place.

The shipwreck is upon you. And there is no going back to the life you had.

The waters that drown are the waters that save.

Before there was a human, there was a sea; there was a watery, shapeless chaos, a blackness that had no form and no meaning. Spirit came and hovered over the black, liquid night of the waters; the dove brooded over the anarchy we call sea. And she stayed there long enough, breathed into her deep enough, for life to come up shimmering out of the ocean. It is these primordial waters that we come from, the same water that poured out of the woman you called mother in the hours before you were born. It is into these dark waters that you must return, into this primitive abyss, into this watery grave. You must return again to the chaos of the world you knew before you started trying to build a world you could control—back to the bottom of the ocean where you once lay, submerged.

In secular terms, we call this phenomenon "drowning"; in the Christian tradition, we call it "baptism."

The bad news is that this shipwreck feels like death, because you really may be dying. The bad news is that old and familiar things you loved and that made you what you were are slowly passing away. The good news is you're being born, and this drowning makes possible the moment when all things become new—most of all, you.

Maybe a preacher on the radio told you once you could be born again if you just repeated a prayer after him. How I wish this were so. But the Scripture where a man named Nicodemus comes under cloak of night for a secret rendezvous with Jesus, and the prophet speaks to him about being born again, is also the place where Jesus talks about that Spirit, the one who broods over the sea, bringing life and beauty out of chaos. The Spirit is like the wind, he says; you don't know where it comes from—and you don't know where it is going. And the people who say yes to this undomesticated Spirit, the people who say yes to the wind—yes to the sea—will be like this Spirit, not knowing where they came from, or where they are going. They are people who learn to trust the wind instead of fighting it, people who learn to navigate the chaos rather than eliminate it. They will be people born of Spirit, people born of the violence of the storm and the wildness of the wind. And because the Spirit who enters them is the Spirit of life itself, they will live forever.

You can't descend back into the waters of your mother's womb, the prophet tells Nicodemus. But you can be born again; you can be made new. It's just that when you do, it won't be because you made "a decision for Jesus," because you prayed the magic prayer. If you wish to become someone and something else entirely than the you that was before the storm came . . . you will have to peer into the sea that threatens to swallow you whole, dive into the mouth of it—and trust. You will have to let God happen to you, which requires letting life happen to you, all the way down. You cannot continue to flail your arms, beat against the sea, and damn the waves. You have to let yourself go all the way under—into the depths of God, into the depths of your own soul, into the depths, of life itself.

You will have to linger at the ocean floor, where the sea monsters live, and confront everything in you that you've constructed a whole life out of avoiding. You will have to confront the mysteries that lie in the bottom of you. Just in case you are, in fact, drowning and don't feel like you can quite hold out for another hundred pages or more, I'll give you one spoiler: Love is the mystery at the bottom of all the others. To almost everyone's surprise, until an invisible hand holds them underwater long enough, the most beautiful things in all of creation are down here— below, beneath, under the world you knew.

These very waters that are now drowning you have the life-giving power of Spirit within them, deep beneath the current. The waters that drag you down where you do not wish to go—if you do not resist them—will spit you out like Jonah, spewed out of the belly of the whale. And you will burst out of the waters the second time, just like you did the first—screaming in terror; shimmering in your sea-soaked, new skin; glad to be out; terrified to be here . . . yet so wonderfully alive and breathing and so terribly hopeful, no longer encumbered by the things that once dragged you down.

> The Spirit whispers into the pitch-black that surrounds you, carrying the words Jesus spoke to Nicodemus in the wind: You must be born again.

The waters that drown you are the same waters that will save you; and the same sea that is pulling you under is the sea that will make you new. The things you've been holding on to cannot keep you afloat any longer. There is no going back down the birth canal when the Spirit of life is pushing you forward, despite yourself. The only way to lose yourself forever is to keep hanging on to the life you had before. The storm rides you hard, but the Spirit whispers into the pitch-black that surrounds you, carrying the words Jesus spoke to Nicodemus in the wind:

You must be born again.

Holy Ghost Stories

Letting the storm and the night have their way with you, letting the Spirit come in with the wind to make you into something new, is much easier said than done. There are so many reasons not to be reborn. There are so many reasons to choose resuscitation over resurrection. There is nothing quite so scary as the Holy Ghost, because we intuitively know that to make room for this Spirit is to make room for our own upending. Rather than give ourselves over to the whims of that Ghost, it seems at first easier to choose to live as ghosts ourselves. After my own shipwreck, I tried my hand at this for a while.

It was a cold Friday night in my hometown of Charlotte, North Carolina, when I went to the neighborhood bar with my friends who used to work at the church I had founded nine years before. They were still my friends, but I was not their pastor anymore, or anyone of consequence, or anyone—so it felt—in particular. I was on the long side of my own shipwreck, no longer what I was, but altogether unclear on what it was I was becoming. I remember how much I enjoyed the familiar comfort of my friends that night, our easy conversation, and our deep belly laughs. I remember it being one of the rare moments when I enjoyed not being a pastor, enjoyed not doing my best Jesus of Nazareth impression. I liked being a real boy for a few minutes—in a neighborhood bar with friends who stood by me.

That was until my friend Blake told me she saw a girl who used to go to our church playing pool on the other side of the room. The girl, Sarah, was an artist in our town, a friend I had lost track of. But her hair was different, and I told Blake this was not the same girl—which gave way to a bet of sorts and ended with Blake going over to talk to her. And yes, it was the same girl, who had also been glancing over her shoulder our way, trying to figure out if this was her former pastor here in the bar.

So she came over to say hello. I remember feeling a little self-conscious, holding the drink in my hand. For the sake of my mother, I am inclined to want to say I was drinking a Coke—which does have the benefit of being exactly one-half true! So when Sarah came over breezily, I felt myself stiffen just a little. After all, I had baptized her.

All those days for me were marked by the tension of clinging to my old life, a way of wearing a child's floaties in the raging sea and telling myself I was not drowning. I was becoming more and more aware that the life I was living was a half-life, at best.

I used to have a stable marriage, lead a thriving church, and have what felt like an infinite number of friends.

But all that had changed.

In six separate conversations in the three days prior to going to the bar that night, I told people close to me the exact same thing—that the closest thing to a job I had today was being the former pastor of the church I founded and led. I said I felt like the ghost of who I used to be—the pastor of Renovatus.

I used to be the pastor of a thriving church my wife and I planted—a church for liars, dreamers, and misfits. I used to lead this community that was all about love and people and beauty and justice. I used to have a strong marriage to a wife I both admired and adored. I used to be a rising star in my native denomination where my father and grandfather had been pastors. My dad, semiretired, lived ten minutes away and had an office at the church as our volunteer missions pastor. I was living the dream.

I had lived a life that did not deviate from the script I was handed. I loved people the best I knew how. For whatever other shortcomings I had, I had sincerity for days. At our church, we had not built a Christian Walmart; we built counterculture. It was all about the ideas and the people and doing what we did for the sheer love of a thing. Once, while on a mission trip to a Palestinian school we supported, some kids were pointing at me, laughing and saying, "He looks just like Jesus from the video!" I hoped I lived like him too.

But I was not that person anymore.

I had failed in my marriage. I had failed my church. I had failed my friends. I sailed my own ship into the rocks—and both the relationships that mattered most to me and my calling to the church I loved were the casualties.

At thirty-six years old, I was living at my parents' house, ghostwriting for other Christian leaders on my laptop on a folding card table in the utility building where my dad kept his train set. Awash with self-loathing and grief, I was on a descent, and I knew it full well. Only occasionally did I come up for air, to haunt my hometown as a shadow of the man I used to know. Everyone else around me seemed alive enough, and even moving on with their lives, except for me—I was in a cover band, wearing my old clothes, playing the greatest hits of a man who had long since departed.

I was shipwrecked.

I could not go back to the life I had before, but felt incapable of stepping into a new one. I thought often of the verse where Jesus said he saw Satan fall like lightning.[2] But our human falling isn't usually like that—quickly. Most of us fall slowly, hitting every step on the way down—or at least that's what I was doing. Unable to sort out the complicated emotional tangle of my most primal relationships, I had taken myself out of ministry to the people I loved, unresolved, and was wandering around, the ghost of my former self, trying to figure out what to do next.

So this is the space I'm occupying while I chat it up with Sarah, catching up broadly about our lives. I thought it was pleasant enough, but Sarah gave me odd looks, like she could not figure me out somehow, while I was perfectly polite, in my perfectly pastorally trained way. At one point, she laughed, and I asked her why she was laughing, "I don't know, Jonathan. You just . . . still seemed like 'Pastor Jonathan' when you walked in here tonight." I didn't exactly know what to make of this, but a few minutes later, she ambled back over to finish a game of pool with her friends, and I went back to talking with mine.

Until just before I was getting ready to leave, when she came back over a second time and asked if she could talk to me once more. So I waved my friends on and sat down next to her on a barstool. I remembered Sarah as being an intuitive person, as someone who I would have said "walked in the Spirit." And this time when she talked, there was a kind of intensity in her eyes, the wild look I saw on the faces of traveling evangelists as I grew up in rural

Pentecostal churches in the South—the look that said the Holy Ghost had taken over.

She said, "Jonathan, I feel like I need to tell you something, but I don't want to offend you. When you walked in here tonight, I was really happy to see you. I was really excited to come over and talk to you and just find out how you're doing and what you're up to these days. But I wasn't excited by the time I walked away from you. I don't know how to put it—you know I think you are a brilliant writer, and your preaching has made such a huge impact on my life. I don't know exactly where you are now or what all you are feeling. But it's like wherever you are right now—you don't know how to really be here. Like you don't know how to own being in a broken place. It's like you still feel the need to put on, like you are the pastor of the church. I think there is so much in you to say and to write that only you can say and write. But it's all going to be a blazing sham if it doesn't come from a truthful place—if it doesn't come from the place you are right here, right now. It's like you don't know how to be comfortable in your own skin. If you like being here in the bar with your friends, that's okay—but be here, be wherever you are now."

Sarah would interrupt herself over and over, apologizing for being so forward, which I waved off. I can recognize the voice of the Spirit, just as much in a bar, and I was entirely open to all that was said. I was hungry to feel seen and known by God, somehow, in my one-foot-in-the-grave, in-between life. It was exactly the feeling I had been describing to my friends. I felt like Bruce Willis at the end of *The Sixth Sense*—that all these things were happening to me and around me; I just didn't know I was the one already dead.

Toward the end, Sarah looked off for a second, pensively, before staring back at me again with the eyes of a prophetess, whatever Spirit had emboldened her: "The best way I'd know how to say it, Jonathan—and I don't want to hurt your feelings!—is that when you walked in the door here tonight, it's like it wasn't Jonathan Martin who walked in the door; it was the ghost of the pastor of Renovatus."

Had I ever heard God speak to me quite so clearly? No wonder when I walked into the bar, Sarah thought she saw a ghost. I was hovering between two worlds, tethered to neither.

Your Faith Will Not Fail, Even When You Do

During that storied final meal Jesus shared with his disciples, only hours away from all the torments that awaited him, there is an extraordinary exchange between Jesus and Peter. The truly remarkable thing is that this is just before Jesus tells Peter he will disown him. Sitting at the table, where the peculiar alchemy of wine turning to blood and bread becoming body was already at play, Jesus looks across the table at the fiery, well-intentioned disciple whose face was not yet shadowed by the guilt of betrayal. And he speaks words of heartbreaking tenderness to the man who says he will die for Jesus but will in actuality curse him by morning: "Simon, Simon, listen! Satan has demanded to sift all of you like wheat, but I have prayed for you that your own faith may not fail; and you, when once you have turned back, strengthen your brothers."[3]

Satan has desired to sift you like wheat, says the man who Roman soldiers will carve up like cattle in just a few hours. But even knowing the physical and psychological torture that he will soon endure, Jesus' concern is for Peter—that he will not be able to live with himself after what he is about to do. He knows the storm of bitter tears, the stomach-churning agony of regret that will eat him from the inside for betraying the one he loved the most. He knows the sting of it could rend Peter's mind, the way the whip will soon rend his own skin. So he says, "I have prayed for you—that your faith may not fail."

Objectively, conclusively, decisively—Peter himself will fail before the rooster crows. That is already established. But while Peter will fail spectacularly, on the surface of things, there is something at work in him that is deeper than his failure. The waves will overtake the man and his blustering ego, but in the depths of the sea within Peter is a stronger, more ancient current that did not originate from him—a current that need not be shaken by his failure on the surface: his faith. I have prayed for you, Peter, that even though you will fail (in fact, be known for the most famous failure in the history of the church), your faith will not fail. The tsunami will come, and take your self-reliance and your pride; humiliation will wash over you. You will fail, but I have prayed for you . . . that your failure would not destroy your faith but deepen it. I have prayed for you that the very thing that was intended to kill you will make the faith already planted in the deepest soil of you even stronger.

It is possible to fail, and not have our faith fail us. It is possible to lose our lives, and not lose our souls. The master teacher taught us himself that it is only in losing our lives—in their ego pretensions and posturing, in their careful image constructions and neediness—that this richer, deeper, below-the-surface life can be found. This is the life hidden with Christ in God, where almost anything can happen at the top of things without disrupting the grace that lies in the bottom of the sea in you. This is the place in the depths where you can be cut off from your very self (as you understood it), and from the name your father gave you, and from the place where you grew up, and from the tribe that gave you language, and from the story that gave you meaning—only to find that nothing can separate you from the love of God.

> It is possible to fail, and not have our faith fail us. It is possible to lose our lives, and not lose our souls.

When the storm is still brewing over the waters, and the sky sickens into an ominous gray-black, and you feel the electric charge in the air in your very skin, inevitably the question comes: Will I survive this? Can I make it through the storm that is coming (whatever sent it here, and however it came)? And of course, there are many storms fierce enough to toss you, throw you, destabilize you, and scare you that do not result in shipwreck. Some storms last only for the night; some pockets of violent air are only turbulence.

But some storms are more violent, more relentless, more

exacting. Some winds will not be calmed; some floods will not be dammed until they have their way with you, until they walk away with their pound of flesh. And whether or not, again, the storm finds its origin in the undomesticated wildness of nature and of created things—or whether or not the storm originates in you—does not change the scope or scale or power of it. The storms that come will test us all, and it is entirely possible one comes to you that will end in your failure before the wind and waves recede. But the Spirit in the wind whispers the words of Jesus again, inserting your own name for Simon's: "I have prayed for you that your own faith may not fail—and even when you do . . . that your faith may even grow stronger through your failure."

During my own shipwreck, my long season of descent, I returned over and over to the story in Acts 27 of Paul's shipwreck. The apostle was a prisoner in transport when God revealed to him that a storm was coming. Because Paul knows the Spirit, he is a man in tune with matters of wind and wave as much as the matters of the soul; and he knows the boat he is traveling on will soon encounter a terrible storm. Before the storm comes, he tells his captor companions a heartening thing: "None of you will lose a hair from your heads."[4] The good news is, you are not going to die. The bad news is, the boat that has been carrying you—the vessel that had taken you from port to port, place to place, the strong and stable boat that made you feel safe on all the oceans you've sailed thus far—the boat will be lost. They were not going to lose their lives, but they were going to lose the boat.

Losing the boat is no small thing. To lose the boat is to lose the ground beneath your feet, the stories you told yourself and others, to lose what protected you from all the elements before. To lose the boat is to lose everything that kept you afloat before, to be thrown into the vast and merciless sea now alone, with nothing left to protect you from its moody tides, the blazing sun above it, or the black-eyed creatures that lurk beneath it. You can lose your boat, lose your house with all the pictures inside it, lose your job, lose your most defining relationship.

And still not lose you.

And still not lose your soul.

And still not lose your faith.

Make no mistake: You will be stripped down in the shipwreck. But you will not be lost.

While I would not recommend a shipwreck to anyone, any more than I would recommend cancer, car accidents, or the plague, I can yet attest to a mysterious truth I have since heard over and over from people who have survived their own shipwrecks: On the other side of them, there is a stronger, deeper, richer, more integrated life. That on the other side of the storm that tears you to pieces is a capacity to love without doubt, to live without fear, to be something infinitely more powerful than the man or woman you were before it happened. Almost nobody who survives a shipwreck would ever sign up to do it all over again, a second time. Nobody can exactly say they were glad it happened. And yet repeatedly, I hear people say the same remarkable thing—that they also under no circumstances would choose to go back and be the person they were before. Nobody would choose to lose the loved one all over again to the unexpected illness, or lose the job they trained for years to get, or lose the relationship they invested heart and soul into for half of their adult life.

I cannot tell you with any degree of confidence that you will not fail your test. I cannot tell you with any degree of certainty that your ship is going to make it out in one piece. Like Job, I am a small man, unable to sort the elements of God and cosmos and good and evil, of human freedom and responsibility, of divine will, or of the unadorned chaos that is the sea itself.

I can only align myself with the greater wisdom of the Teacher and of his apostle and tell you that even though you might fail—utterly—your faith does not have to. I can tell you that even if the ship does not survive, you will.

Storms come, as do a legion of demons that come for the sifting. Take heart; Jesus says, "I have prayed for you."

Chapter Two

How Not to Survive a Shipwreck

*Because I'm a Karamazov. Because when I
fall into the abyss, I go straight into it, head
down and heels up, and I'm even pleased
that I'm falling in just such a humiliating
position, and for me I find it beautiful.*

Fyodor Dostoyevsky, *The Brothers Karamazov*

*The world breaks everyone, and afterward
many are strong at the broken places.*

Ernest Hemingway

On the front page of the Swedish newspaper, underneath a picture of awkward, oversized me stuck in a tiny Volkswagen wedged between two walls in a back alley, was this quote: "'I got my own drama,' said Martin, a Bergman enthusiast."

If they only knew.

I can tolerate almost any sort of discomfort without too much complaint—as long as I am not embarrassed. The collective dream we humans have of showing up to middle school wearing only our underwear has a powerful grip over our imagination. I don't want to be something bad, or feel something bad . . . if I can avoid it. Just not nearly as much as I don't want to ever have to look bad in front of other people. Yet in this season of my life, I've had to stare down the monster of humiliation over and over again.

Several months after I left the church, I was in worse shape than ever, but couldn't bear the appearance of a man spiraling down as much as I was. So as upside-down as I felt, I began my fumbling attempts at engaging the world again—which took me to Sweden.

My first time back in the pulpit felt like some kind of chemistry experiment. With all my preaching muscles rusty, I was flying to Sweden to speak ten times in less than a week. As out of rhythm as I was, the prospect of speaking in a country I had not visited to people I did not know sounded daunting; and yet there was a sense of adventure to it too. That trip was also significant in that it was the first time I had attempted to do a major international speaking trip alone. To put it mildly, I am challenged at finding my way around new places (as well as old ones, really . . . I have no sense of direction). But I had steeled myself for this trip. Sure, I felt fragile, like my bones were all glass—but I still had the fire in my belly, and that had served me well enough before.

I had planned to do some sightseeing around Sweden for a few days before my first speaking gig. As it turned out, I was going to be there over "Ingmar Bergman Weekend," a whole weekend of festivities built around the life and work of the famous Swedish director on the tiny island of Fårö, where Bergman lived the second half of his life. Entering the second half of my own, stumbling not strutting, I was ecstatic about the opportunity. I've been a huge fan of Bergman's bleak spiritually and intellectually provocative films all my adult life. The prospect of visiting the locations where his films were shot, the places he lived and played—as well as the Bergman Center itself—was intoxicating. It was good to feel really excited about anything in my life again . . . it felt like it had been such a long time.

There were a number of issues surrounding the flight, and I slept very little on the way to Stockholm. But my excitement was undeterred. By the time I boarded the tiny plane in Stockholm to go to the medieval town of Wisby, where I would then rent a car to take to Fårö, I had been awake for more than twenty-four hours. But having a new adventure in an unknown land was intoxicating however discombobulated I felt. When I got the rental car, I noted it was a manual—I drive an automatic back home. I had not driven one in a few years, but I figured I could get the hang of it. Besides, I was ready to be on my way.

So using my phone's GPS to guide me, I set out in the little Volkswagen, bright and eager, like it was my first day of school. You could practically hear Tom Petty's "Free Fallin'" in your head, even with the radio off. It felt like I was in a movie about starting your life over and finding hope again. My pain so fresh, I wanted to fast-forward into resurrection and hoped desperately this trip might be the start of it somehow. As I got into the little town of Wisby, the roads got tinier—these were cobblestone streets built in the 1100s. Almost everything was one-way. But my "Spidey sense" was too tired to be tingling. I kept following the GPS.

Siri guided me down an especially tiny side street that went through an alley and down a hill. The farther I got down, the more it felt like the walls were closing in on me, like I was in a scene from *Alice in Wonderland*. Jet lag is a very real thing, and I thought it explained my little mini–head trip. I was near the bottom of the hill when it became painfully clear this was not an optical illusion—the street was actually getting narrower. You could barely get a bicycle through the outlet at the bottom.

That's when I knew I was in trouble. I had not yet had to put the car in reverse, and I couldn't figure out how. So whenever I tried to back the car up, I would slowly inch even farther . . . and farther . . . down the hill. But of course I had to let up on the clutch to try it at all, so I just kept going farther down—until I was completely wedged between the two stone walls. *Wedged*. As in, the side mirrors were collapsed in, and there was literally no way to even crack my door open. I was completely stuck. I could not back up, and there was no way out of the car for the time being except by breaking the front windshield. *I can't believe this is happening*, I thought.

Along with a string of really innovative, fatigue-induced obscenities.

You have to understand—my greatest fear traveling anywhere internationally is playing the role of "the stupid American." I am not going to be the obnoxious, demanding American—I *do* have control over that. But I'm terrified of looking foolish in another culture. As I'm sitting there, big guy in a little Volkswagen, some people walked out of a pub on the corner and saw me. I was paralyzed. What should I do? Should I try to get their attention? How would I even know exactly what to ask for at this point? My brain and body were tired—I couldn't think straight. As I'm feeling my cheeks turn deeper hues of red from embarrassment, trying to figure out how I might escape, they pull out their iPhones—and start taking pictures of me. While laughing. They went back into the pub and got more friends—who also took pictures. As the minutes passed, a whole crowd of onlookers gathered. And I'm not making this up—why would I? By the time it was all said and done, at least thirty people had taken pictures with their cell phones of the stupid American trapped in his car.

By the time I was done with my two weeks in Sweden, I could honestly say its people were the gentlest, sweetest people on earth. In fact, I would go as far as to call it my favorite country I've ever visited. The people I met were delightful, like they were out of a storybook. I was all but ready to become a citizen by the time I left. I want to *live* in Stockholm, with all its old-world charm and new-world fashions. But in that moment, on no sleep, mostly incredulous at myself for not being able to even get to the hotel without my first mishap—I hated everyone in that godforsaken country. I cursed IKEA, Swedish meatballs, their fabulous health care, and even that rotten Swedish chef. I decided I would sell my white Volvo when I got home. It was the one and only moment of my life I ever wanted to wear camouflage, join the NRA, and drink beer while listening to Lee Greenwood's "God Bless the USA."

Finally a really nice man came out from the pub and tried to help me. Unable to tell me how to get the car in reverse, he called a tow truck. About eighty minutes later, the tow truck came, and I was back to loving Ingmar Bergman art films, streamlined modern furniture, Scandinavian luxury in automobiles, and universal health care—even for animals. I was back to wanting to marry the country of Sweden.

But here is the kicker: While the tow truck driver was hooking up the cable to the car, another man came around the corner with a large professional camera with a really long lens. He was from the local paper. I saw a copy the next morning, and sure enough—there was a picture of me trapped in the car in the alley on the front page. Translated from Swedish, "Oh no, not again: American tourist stuck in alley." That's right. Less than twenty-four hours into my trip, and I made the front page for being the stupid American. The reporter asked me why I was in Sweden—and I was not about to tell him I was there to preach in churches and lecture in seminaries. "I'm here for Ingmar Bergman Weekend," I said. Hence the last line of the article, "Martin, a Bergman enthusiast, says, 'I got my own drama.'"

That scene felt like an allegory for my whole life in this season: feeling helpless, exposed, foolish, dependent, unable to move at all on my own—having to rely on other people to come and pull me out of where I was. Just when I thought the shipwreck might be over, and I imagined myself strong enough to pick myself up and make some brilliant comeback, I ran smack into the reality that I could not do it on my own.

Too often in the wake of a shipwreck, we think all we need to do is push ahead, to keep moving forward. But when we do that too quickly, too self-assuredly, we find ourselves like I did—an awkward American in a tiny car in an even tinier alley—stuck. Not only that, but we find ourselves suddenly reliant on others to get us unstuck.

It was a painfully embarrassing lesson for me to learn: You just don't survive a shipwreck by pushing forward as if everything is fine.

I had never felt more incompetent. I was no longer the guy calling the shots, giving advice, saving the day—I was the one in need of saving. If I could not find some people who could come along and pull me, I was hopeless. I got myself stuck. I had no way out.

That's what happens when we try to fast-forward our own redemption; when we think we can stage that brilliant comeback all on our own.

I was no longer bringing people to Jesus by the carload. I was the lame man on the mat, in need of someone else to carry me to Jesus.

The Path of Salvation Is the Path of Humiliation

What if God doesn't choose to save us in spite of our failures, losses, and embarrassments, but precisely through them? What if it is not avoiding falling that strengthens our faith, but the falling itself? Before the shipwreck, we still maintain illusions of our control. So long as we still think we are in charge of our lives, there is no space for God—we are still clinging to life. It is only when our hands are too weak to cling to life anymore—because of sickness, death, addiction, failure—that we can find life. This is what Jesus means when he says we have to lose our lives to find them. That's not a metaphor for "giving up a lot to follow Jesus."

It's not a metaphor for anything. It's a way of saying what it sounds like: The only way to find God is through losing.

> What if God doesn't choose to save us in spite of our failures, losses, and embarrassments, but precisely through them?

It is not some strange quirk of the tale between Jesus and Peter that God chooses and uses Peter "despite" his failure. The reason his faith won't fail is precisely because Peter did in fact fail—and it put him flat on his back. There is no walking into the kingdom of God, or into the grace of God. We can only be carried, like the paralyzed man whose friends brought him to Jesus in Mark 2. Peter was going to be put in a position to bring strength to his brothers, not because he avoided falling, but because he did fall—and thus encountered the Jesus who held on to him, in the letting go.

Yet for Peter, even this was not all. During his sweet reunion with Jesus on the other side of resurrection, right after Jesus asked Peter if he loved him, Jesus told him, "When you were younger you dressed yourself and went where you wanted; but when you are old . . . someone else will dress you and lead you where you do not want to go."[1] Peter just found out how right Jesus is in his predictions when he denied knowing Jesus, like he was told he would. Now he is being told that more humiliation awaits him. What is more humiliating than not being able to take care of your own most basic bodily needs—to be unable to pick out your own clothes, dress yourself, go to the bathroom, decide where it is you want to go? Yet even so, this is not some punishment for Peter because of his disowning Jesus.

Peter has to get even more familiar with humiliation, because God trusts him with the biggest job in the world—to be the first leader of the early church, the rock on whom the movement would be founded. For a calling so weighted, no one could be trusted who was not well acquainted with humiliation. The very things that make Peter weak are the very things that make him dependent—no longer captive to the posturing bravado of a runaway ego ("Don't worry, Jesus—I would *never* deny knowing you!"). Now he will no longer be a man beholden to big, grand gestures—he will be small enough, fragile enough, to break free of all the old illusions of control. His grip on his whole life will become loose enough and weak enough, to where he's not capable of clinging to anything anymore. Thus, God can finally trust him with the keys to the family car.

> The path to salvation is the path of humiliation.

It is only when we are no longer in control—because of sickness, death, or our own bad choices—that we no longer cling. The path to salvation is the path of humiliation.

The Grace of Dependence

I do not like this any more than you do. I'm aware it might sound like overstatement, or shock and awe, and it is at best inelegant as a theological construct. Thankfully, this doesn't matter, since God doesn't use theology to save anyone—just humiliation. The worst enemy any one of us has is not some kind of literal Satan (though I do believe there is a force of evil at work in the world that is greater than the sum of its parts), but our own egos. The ego is not evil per se, but illusory—who we perceive ourselves to be as opposed to who we really are. Salvation is baptism into reality, out of the world of illusions, delusions, ideas, and ideals. Salvation is an immersion into the real.

The truth at the dirt-floor bottom of us is that we are weak, dependent, and small—but infinitely loved. This has always been true. But the necessary ego-building project we begin at infancy, crucial to our survival through childhood, adolescence, and even early adulthood, is a massive cover-up wherein we attempt to convince everyone—most of all, ourselves—that we are stronger than we look. The ego gives us a layer of protection. It keeps us from being utterly crushed by many of the external forces of pain and rejection that might otherwise destroy us. But this necessary insulation of ego, the padding that keeps us from having to confront the world from our deepest, truest self, is the very thing that kills us over time.

From our earliest memories, we've been on a lifelong search to differentiate from the people around us, based on our judgments. Because I like this food, this book, this film, this god, this sports team, and not any of the others—I know who I am. It gives us a sense of separateness, of set-apartness, of individuation. The trouble is, we are not nearly as separate, as set apart, or as individual as we think we are. We are bound together by our common, shared dependence; our fragility; and our need. "We men and women are all in the same boat, upon a stormy sea. We owe to each other a terrible and tragic loyalty," G. K. Chesterton writes.[2] But the ego conspires against this truth, convincing us we are different; we are special; we are not like everyone else.

We can only be saved through the demolition of these lies, and the only means powerful enough to demolish them is humiliation. This is why it is so crucial that God saves the world through his own humiliation—the humiliation of the cross. And why Jesus taught then that the only way we could be his disciples is to take up our own crosses and follow him. This is not a matter of saying, "I want the cross." In fact, it is fairly rare that any of the true crosses we have to carry are crosses we would choose for ourselves. They feel imposed on us, largely outside of our control, which is what makes them so uniquely gruesome.

At all costs, we want to avoid feeling ourselves as the ones in need, feeling dependent on God and others. We prefer to feel ourselves to be strong and self-reliant. But self-reliance is always a kind of denial, a refusal to see the brazen truth of how contingent our lives are on other lives, on nature, on the world. We are far more interconnected than we care to admit, more drastically shaped by the lives of others and more significant to others than we know.

Our sense of individuality and self-sufficiency is a survival mechanism established on a lie—that we are autonomous.

This is really what the ancient biblical narrative of Adam and Eve partaking of the tree of the knowledge of good and evil is all about. They are deceived into believing that if they partake of the tree, they will be able to separate themselves from God by their own moral judgments. They are looking for a way to escape their native dependence. It is actually a necessary part of the human journey to partake of the fruit, to attempt to individuate and separate ourselves from others. Ego development is essential to help us grow up and get out the door. But there is a force of destiny, of inevitability, that this project runs its course—and that in the end, we find out we are not nearly as "other" as we thought we were. One way or the other, through illness, divorce, calamity, or death, we will be stripped away from the things that made us feel other than/apart from our fellow humans. And life itself will plunge us into the sea of our own shared humanity.

Ideally, the primary function of religion will be to loose us from our illusions of individuality and self-reliance and deliver us from the toxic fruit of ego development. But instead of equipping us to avoid the tree of the knowledge of good and evil, we make entire religions out of worshiping around the tree instead. Rather than breaking down the illusory boundaries of "us" and "them," insiders and outsiders, sacred and profane, religion often underwrites these boundaries, reinforces them, gives us a sense of being good guys over/against the bad guys. Instead of subverting the lie of "us" and "them," religion is often a tool to make us feel special, set apart. No wonder Jesus tells the Pharisees of his time, practitioners of these kinds of judgments, that they make converts "twice as much a child of hell as yourselves."[3] "Us and them" religion is poison to the soul, and it often takes a lifetime of humiliation to detoxify us from it.

In the Christian tradition, those who are most immersed in the experiential reality of God always come to moments of illumination, where they are able to see through the deception of insider/outsider, white hat/black hat religion, and see the essential unity between humans. Thomas Merton famously devoted himself to the monastic life, often feeling set apart by his devout practices. But for Merton, the defining moment of his adult life was this epiphany he had while standing on a street corner:

> In Louisville, at the corner of Fourth and Walnut, in the center of the shopping district, I was suddenly overwhelmed with the realization that I loved all those people, that they were mine and I theirs, that we could not be alien to one another even though we were total strangers. It was like waking from a dream of separateness, of spurious self-isolation in a special world, the world of renunciation and supposed holiness. The whole illusion of a separate holy existence is a dream . . . There is no way of telling people that they are all walking around shining like the sun . . . I suddenly saw the secret beauty of their hearts, the depths of their hearts where neither sin nor desire nor self-knowledge can reach, the core of their reality, the person that each one is in God's eyes.

If only they could all see themselves as they really *are*.
If only we could see each other that way all the time.[4]

I think mystics like Merton, because of the amount of time and attention they give to their interior lives, are often able to arrive at these epiphanies faster than the rest of us—if they don't allow their own sense of consecration, of otherness, to sabotage them from such revelations. We do not easily or often arrive at these moments where we see each other in God's eyes, where we see ourselves as we really are—see that "they were mine and I was theirs, that we could not be alien to one another even though we were total strangers." But one way or the other, we do get to this place of simple, clear perspective, where all the posturing and bluster around our uniqueness and individuality is burned away.

Friends in Low Places

I was entering the humiliation of going from the one who served to the one who had to be served, of going from the one who carried to the one in need of carrying. The sheer extent of need in me felt bottomless. I'd heard about the underside of life from my friends, and I trusted their accounts. I had never exactly gone looking, at least consciously, to bear witness myself. But looking back, I think it was what my soul wanted, even when everything else in me would have protested the descent that would have made possible such a way of seeing.

Flat on my back, I'd have gone nowhere if I wouldn't have been able to look up into the faces of my friends. Dr. Chris Green is one of my best friends, the brother I never had. He, like me, grew up in a conservative Pentecostal environment, went on a similarly odd academic journey, and reclaimed his passion for his native tradition in a similarly odd way. Chris is one of the only people in the world capable of making me feel less odd. When we met for the first time several years ago for a dinner, it was like finding the brother I never had, as an only child. I felt like he somehow understood the darkness and the ambiguity in me, while we were both getting light from a lot of the same places too. So much of my best work and deepest reflections have come out of our marathon conversations, which are the theological version of jazz musicians in a jam session. There is no way I could have come to see all the things I've come to see about God and faith without his companionship on this long, slow walk to Emmaus.

In the life before the shipwreck, I could at least have some small sense of having something to offer the people I cared for. When Chris and I first met, he told me beautiful things about what my sermons meant to him while he was navigating a lot of transition in his own life. The extent to which, post-shipwreck, I had to rely on Chris was, frankly, mortifying. That included conversations where he tended to my damaged spirit. But that included more tangible things too, like him driving from Cleveland, Tennessee, where he teaches seminary, to speak at the church every weekend while I was on sabbatical—while dealing with his own health issues, mind you.

Needing such care from my friends made me feel uniquely useless. I remember driving to Cleveland soon after I left the church, to be present for a small surgery Chris was having. The procedure was no big deal, and thus I knew my presence was not actually needed. But the day after the surgery, sitting in the chair in his bedroom, phasing in and out of sleep while reading a novel as Chris rested, was the first time on the other side of any of that I felt remotely useful to anyone. I remember thinking distinctly that I hoped I'd have more opportunities to show my love for the people I cared about by showing up for them, not just preaching to them. From there, so much of my new life even now goes back to Chris's faithful friendship. An awful lot of weight landed on one friend who was willing to put me over his shoulder when I didn't have the strength to walk.

Steven Furtick is one of my oldest friends, and one of my favorite people to be around. He's pure energy, a true man of faith who has mafia-esque loyalty to his friends. Like all my other close relationships, I always felt our friendship had a sort of reciprocity—we share enough of the same passions and yet are different enough to where our conversations have always been among the liveliest and purest fun of any in my life. It always felt like we complement each other and bring perspective to each other that was good for us both—the whole "iron sharpens iron" thing.

Which made it so much worse to feel like I showed up on Steven's doorstep empty-handed—out of reasons and out of answers. There was one night in particular, during the worst of the storm, when he invited me to hang out at his office. And after three hours of soul baring, the way we do, the invitation was extended into a dinner invitation at his house. This was smack-dab in the middle of Steven's biggest challenge in ministry, under a barrage of unexpected media scrutiny. I knew he was reeling from all of it, that he was feeling the weight of all the criticism. And yet, unflinching, he carved out time and space for me.

That night in particular, dinner turned into "why don't you just spend the night?" I can't recall the last time I had spent the night at another adult's house, unless we were on some kind of a trip together. That is the kind of courtesy the old version of me would have always politely declined. But I was on the underside then. And that night in particular, I really didn't know exactly where to go or what to do—the idea of being with my friend and his family was comforting, if still mortifying to feel myself so dependent. I'll never forget going with Steven and his two sons after dinner that night to their championship tee-ball game. To get them pumped up on the way, he gave them a good "dad pep talk" and then turned on a Jay Z song I happened to love (if you are worried about the children, rest your minds—it was the edited version)—with the four of us rapping along in the car. For just a few moments, it took me outside myself. Those moments were so hard to come by then. After I left the church, he even made space for me to do some contract work for him and the church, consulting on sermons. Of course, I was not comfortable being on the receiving end of such kindness from my friends! And yet I could feel that the ways they served and cared for me was shifting things inside me that needed to be shifted.

But of course, seeing life from the underside didn't just

give me a new perspective with which to see my friends; I was getting a whole new perspective from which to see the world—now not from the head of the table, deciding who's in or who's out, who's up or who's down, but as the one in need.

Nobody survives a shipwreck on their own. When your ship goes under, there are a handful of people in your life who will stay with you. It's no time for saving face or maintaining credibility—it's time to put real weight down on somebody else who can help carry you. Let your ego drown in the watery grave. The only way you have of saving yourself is to let someone outside of you do the saving.

The Grace in Dying

Whatever is death for the ego is liberation for the soul. Often this happens through the process of literal biological death. Kathryn Dowling Singh's magnificent book *The Grace in Dying* illustrates this beautifully. A PhD hospice worker, Singh has devoted her life to being with people through the process of death. From her many hours with the dying, she comes to the extraordinary conclusion that for those who have time to die, there is an astonishing grace on the death process itself. While at first it is fought and resisted, body and soul are forced to become more at home in dependence and need as we lose the capacity to care for ourselves—the death of the ego, the liberation of the true self. Thus it is common, whether it is experienced for a season or only for a few moments toward the end, for people near death to testify to a place of ultimate serenity, peace, and clarity. With no more strength or will for the ego to cling to, there is a purer, truer way of being alive—en route to the passage of death. But unfortunately, it is often not until the process of physical death that we are able to receive these gifts, this graced perspective. We continue instead to work hard to show we are better, holier, apart from someone we deem lesser than us, and we establish nearly all of our sense of self on this sense of otherness.

Unless, of course, it were possible to learn to live with the quality of the dying while we are still alive. This is the promise and peril of authentic Christianity—losing our lives to find them. This is the meaning of taking up the cross, and embracing the grace of death and humiliation, before the deathbed. When we live in this kind of exposure and vulnerability, fully accepting the limits of our humanity and therefore able to embrace others in their own clunky humanness, death no longer holds power over us. When we allow ourselves to live dependent, contingent, yet no longer clinging to anything in particular for a sense of self or individuality, we are living the life of freedom. In not being able to care for ourselves, we are no longer able to perpetuate the myth of self-reliance and can finally come to realize how much we need one another for care of both our bodies and our souls.

Humiliation, then, will not kill us—but it sure feels like a simulation of death. The loss of control, the loss of autonomy, the sense of helplessness, the fragility that comes with realizing how interconnected we all are—all of this is a deathblow to the ego. The idea that God uses our moments of weakness, exposure, and humiliation to transform us is foolish to our minds and offensive to our pride. Surely there is a more sophisticated path to salvation and wholeness than the path of humiliation—especially for people like us!

No wonder the apostle Paul says that the message of the cross is "foolishness to those who are perishing, but to us who are being saved it is the power of God."[5] Given the implications of this cross for our own bloated egos, no wonder so many of us are attracted to a religion where all you have to do is think Jesus carried the cross for you but not have to carry one for yourself. We would far rather believe correct doctrines about Jesus than to go the way of Jesus, allowing the cross as the tool of our humiliation to let him teach us the grace in dying. And yet perhaps it is only in following Jesus to the cross that we can drink fully and deeply of the cup of freedom he offers.

Into the Pool

The truth is, the extent to which we experience death to self is the extent to which we will experience resurrection. That's what baptism is all about. Dying with Christ so we might be raised with him. But we can't halve either part of the equation.

As part of my own journey into death and resurrection, I wanted to be baptized that Easter Sunday. I think for most Christians, baptism is primarily thought of not as joining our humanity with the humanity of Jesus in the descent into the pool, but as coming up with him, sharing his divinity, partaking of his resurrection. I believe in baptism this way, entirely. But I think I had become a little too used to the rhetoric of power, overcoming, and resurrection. When I was baptized for the second time as an adult, it felt like the weight landed less on the power of resurrection, transcending the boundaries of temporal flesh, and more on being immersed into the

> The extent to which we experience death to self is the extent to which we will experience resurrection.

realities of my own frail flesh, allowing myself to become one with the people I had led as a pastor in our shared humanity. I was going to have to enter more deeply into the human, dying part if I was going to hope to partake of the resurrecting, overcoming part.

Deciding to leave the church I founded was one of the hardest, worst things I have ever done, and I still bear the marks of it now. But it was a dive I knew I had to take. As much as I wanted to continue on the journey of helping others become human in all the ways Jesus was and said they could be, I was going to have to embrace my own humanity—and admit I did not have the strength or grace to experience this kind of transformation while in the context of pastoral work.

It was a terrible thing to meet with our leaders and friends in the church to tell them I was leaving. Some were encouraging, some were hurt, some were angry. But I had been suspended between heaven and earth, or was it earth and hell, for too long, and I knew I could not survive any longer in this in-between space, in this no-man's-land. I could not be the ghost of the pastor of Renovatus any longer, haunting the halls of that office anymore.

I had been preaching my heart out. The sermons were not noble—nobility was not an option from anywhere I was. But the rawness of them was killing me. It is one thing to try to make your pain available to God and others in a vulnerable way as a wound for God to heal others, and I do believe that is how God works. But it is another thing to become an exhibition, to feel like people are watching you like a science experiment. Like when I put my G.I. Joe guys in the microwave when I was a kid as the ultimate torture chamber, just to see what would happen to them (spoiler alert: they caught on fire and melted into a red plastic pool of goo). I loved our people, but I didn't care about doing any of that anymore. Another reason I had to go.

It all felt so strange. I had been in full-time ministry since I was twenty-two years old. I had been thrust immediately into the role of expert on God before I knew anything about God or life or how the world worked, really. Some people thought I was a prodigy as a speaker, but whether or not that was true, I had not had the time or space to develop my own soul. I didn't care anymore about whether or not I was good at any of the things I had set out to do; I just wanted to figure out how to be a human being. I wanted to figure out how to live out of my soul rather than out of my head. I did not want to be separate from anyone else, set apart from anyone else, by virtue of what I did for a living. I wanted to be a real boy.

Barbara Brown Taylor is one of my favorite writers, and

I read her lovely, lyrical *Leaving Church* years before. But knowing I must leave, I reread it, and this time it was like ingesting fire. Her words spoke so hot into my soul that it was like they came down from Sinai. There is one section in particular where Taylor writes about being at a pool party hosted by someone in the church and feeling the ache of being apart from the people there in ways she could not bear. She tells of sitting down with a couple in adjacent rocking chairs, an experience she was never able to enjoy because her priority was always to be with people who were in crisis. She tells about laughing with them while corn is stuck in her teeth. And then the section that undid me:

> After my supper had settled I wandered down to the pool, where I watched swimming children splitting beams of underwater light with their bodies. I had baptized many of them, and I loved seeing them all shrieking and paddling around together in one big pool. Suddenly to my right there was a deeper yell, the sound of scrabbling feet on cement, and then a large plop as a fully clothed adult landed in the water.
>
> I stood back and watched the mayhem that ensued. All around me, people were grabbing people and wrestling them toward the water. The dark night air was full of pool spray and laughter. The kids were going crazy. Several people hunting for potential victims turned toward me, their faces lit with smiles. When they saw who I was they turned away again so that I felt sad instead of glad. Whatever changes were occurring inside of me, I still looked waterproof to them. Like the sick

man in John's gospel, who lay by the pool of Beth-zatha for thirty-eight years because he had no one to put him in when the water stirred up, I watched others plunging in ahead of me. Then two strong hands grabbed my upper arms from behind, and before I knew it I was in the water, fully immersed and swimming in light.

I never found out who my savior was, but when I broke the surface, I looked around at all of those shining people with makeup running down their cheeks, with hair plastered to their heads, and I was so happy to be one of them. If being ordained meant being set apart from them, then I did not want to be ordained anymore. I wanted to be human. I wanted to spit food and let snot run down my chin. I wanted to confess being as lost and found as anyone else without caring that my underwear showed through my wet clothes. Bobbing in that healing pool with all those other flawed beings of light, I looked around and saw them as I had never seen them before, while some of them looked at me the same way. The long wait had come to an end. I was in the water at last.[6]

I love the way Taylor plays with the motif of baptism here. Water is integral to life, to new birth. There has always been a mysterious connection between the sea—in antiquity the place of chaos and mystery—and the void of Genesis 1. There is no new life without passing through the waters, like the Hebrews marching through the Red Sea as God parted them. In the New Testament, there is no new life without joining Jesus in the watery grave. Once again, Christianity is the religion of "going through and not around."

I had talked about these ideas for so long. But when that Easter Sunday came around, my last Sunday at our church, it was finally my turn to jump into the pool. My own baptism, then, wasn't just a way of identifying with Christ in his death and resurrection but also a way of stripping myself of all the props and pretensions that made me seem in any way "other" from the people I had served—the people who had gone before me in the water. It didn't feel so much like a leap into some kind of cosmic victory, but like a plunge into our shared humanity. It was the humiliation that washed away my own illusions of separateness and set-apartness. Whatever the plunge into the abyss was going to mean for me, I was in fact putting my weight down on the hope of some kind of resurrection. But the more immediate meaning was a simpler, more primal human one: I am just like everybody else.

We were never meant to recover from our shipwrecks alone. We were never meant to stage our brilliant comeback, pull ourselves up by our bootstraps, get ourselves unstuck without any help. And the truth is, it's better this way.

Chapter Three

Hold On, Let Go

To let go is to lose your foothold temporarily.
Not to let go is to lose your foothold forever.

Søren Kierkegaard

Even as I hold you, I am letting you go.

Alice Walker

There is a small story late in the book of Acts where the apostle Paul finds himself shipwrecked. It feels like a bit of a minor entry in the broad story of the New Testament canon, not the sort of tale that gets a lot of emphasis in preaching or Sunday school. But it felt like there was some treasure hidden in it I needed to discover somehow. I remember scouring the passage over and over, trying to find something to hold on to.

On one level, I knew my shipwreck was very different from Paul's. It was not his decision to be on a boat to begin with—he had been imprisoned by the Roman government for preaching the gospel and was being transported to another town, still awaiting trial. He was a man subject to the elements and to his enemies, whereas I felt utterly responsible for sailing my ship into the rocks. And yet I also feel a storm is a storm, and a shipwreck is a shipwreck. The main thing I remembered about that story was that Paul and his companions survived, and that was the only thing I knew how to be interested in at that point in my life.

It all started for Paul when a moderate south wind began to blow as the men were about to sail past Crete. But then a violent wind came from the north, crashing down on them from Crete, and the ship could not be turned directly into the wind. So they lost control of the vessel. The storm pounded the ship mercilessly for days. They threw the cargo over, but the storm kept pounding. On the third day, they threw the ship's tackle overboard, but the dark rhythm of the storm did not relent. In a haunting phrase, "When neither sun nor stars appeared for many days, and no small tempest raged, all hope of our being saved was at last abandoned."[1]

And that was where I was. I had tried all the standard maneuvers in the manual—praying, reading, trying to find a friend or therapist who might have a magic word for me. But the storm in me got worse instead of better. I tried to throw some cargo overboard, make minor concessions to the storm, throw out a few things I didn't want anyway. But the storm did not relent. I saw no sun or stars for many days. Swallowed under the canopy of night, neither light nor land was in sight, and I could not shake the feeling in the pit of my stomach that the ship was going to go down, with or without me. In the violence of the storm, there were so many times when I just knew things could not get any worse—and yet the pounding did not stop.

The storm around and within me overwhelmed my

senses, but at that point in my life, I simply could not conceive of life without my ship. I would find out later that the ship is not everything—but it sure felt like it was. You can't really overstate the importance of the ship. The ship is the thing that keeps you afloat, that moves you from one place to the next. The ship is the ground beneath your feet that is firm and secure—everything in your life that is known, familiar—no matter how choppy the waves get beneath you. However you got to wherever you are now, there is a ship that got you there.

And precisely because you have weathered many storms in it, the ship means everything to you. In many ways, it feels like the ship is everything. There was no way I could have become the person I was then, or am now, apart from my marriage and my vocation as pastor of the church I planted. It's understandable, then, how easy it is to make the move from "the ship feels like everything to me" to "the ship is everything to me." The ship on which you ate and drank, laughed and cried, sailed and struggled, is so connected to you that it feels like it is you. That you would not know how to be, or if you could be, in the world without it.

The men on Paul's ship were out of food and had lost heart. But that is when the weathered apostle gives them some good news: The angel of God had appeared to him and told him not to be afraid. The angel said Paul was going to survive the storm, and so would everyone traveling with him. Some sailors were about to escape, but Paul tells them if they don't all stay on the boat, they won't be saved. They were going to have to stick around long enough to endure the horrors yet to come. They were going to have to be fully present and accounted for, for the loss of the ship. They would have to feel it, experience it—the dreaded fear of the soul-black night and raging storm—until the bitter end. They would not lose their lives, but they would have to lose their ship.

And yet the old vessel was not wasted. The structure that carried them from the port would carry them no longer. The ship would not survive as a coherent vessel; it would be torn to shreds. But then there is this crucial detail: When the ship sinks, the men grab planks, boards, tiny remaining fragments of the ship—and those small pieces of the wreckage carry them safely to the shore.

When you are in a shipwreck, the first response is always to grasp desperately for someone or something to hold. It is not calculated, but instinctive—a mad, almost flailing attempt to find something to grip. There may be little left to cling to, but there has to be at least some kind of holding on—even if it is just a tacit agreement within yourself to simply keep on living. In this case, holding on is not a metaphor or an abstraction; it is a way of finding a reason, however strong or flimsy it might be, to survive.

Something inside you wants this, even when you otherwise are altogether uncertain as to whether or not you consciously want to survive. That part of you that kicks and screams to still be here is your soul. The soul does not make a home, on the surface of things, so it has largely stayed out of sight, almost in hiding, the bowed head and quiet eyes of a nun in a convent. You can cover up the soul under layers of duty and obligation—you can muzzle it— making only an occasional appearance in moments of joy or of ecstasy before slinking back into the bottom of you, sleeping through its days—a creature of the shadows.

Until the shipwreck, when the soul reasserts itself. You know it is there, because you can hear it scream and because you can feel it bleed. You almost didn't notice it at all, until you heard the sound of what seemed like your soul, dying. And yet precisely because the soul bears the fingerprints of the Spirit, it does not need any reasons to go on—it was no creature of reason to begin with. It needs no logic to fight back; it needs no will in order to survive. When everything else in and around you is dead or dying, the soul will not yet go quietly. Your soul is not dead yet, just because it decided not to be; it claws its way back up through all the grief, without your consent, like some kind of animal.

You're Still Here

The first things overboard when your ship wrecked were all the reasons you ever had for sailing. And when the life you knew is a life you know no longer, and the ship that took you on a thousand adventures before can no longer even keep you afloat, you are right to wonder if there is anything left worth having.

There used to be so many things that we could not live without! How could you live without this person? How could you live without this job? How could you live without this relationship? How could you live without this house? How could you live without your dignity? How could you live without your good reputation? And then death came to someone you loved, or you lost the job, or you sabotaged the relationship or felt your love sabotaged you, or you suffered public humiliation, or you lost your all-important sense of honor. And you thought you really would die.

There was a part of you, maybe even a really large part of you, that really did. There are some losses that in their way mark you forever, and some things you never get over. And because you loved this person or this life and career you built, or valued your dignity, when the bow broke, everything in you screamed. While the sails were ripping and the boards splitting, you heard the sound of your spirit dying. The life you had was over. But to your own shame, *you* were not over, as much as you may have wanted to be. Maybe like a proud samurai, it seemed the best thing you could do on the other side of the shipwreck was to fall on your own sword and stage a protest against anything you once found beautiful. Because you were so sad. Because you were so guilty. Because you were so scared that in the loss of something outside yourself, you lost your own heart to the sea's black rage.

And then came what might be the worst discovery: You didn't die—not really. You walked away from the accident, whether or not you think you or God or the devil or the fates are somehow responsible for it. You just knew you would die, and at times it felt like something in you did. But not *you*. Not all of you, anyway. The ship may have gone down, but miracle of miracles, you're still here.

Can you remember the first time after the funeral, after you could not bear to eat or drink, that the pangs of hunger overwhelmed you? Did you feel incredulous at yourself, at the animal part of you that still wanted food after such a thing? What about when there was a particular taste you wanted, because it was a taste that on some level you actually desired? However much fog, however much sorrow, however much grief—the experience of loss may have altered your taste buds forever. But it hardly killed them.

You watched dreams you cradled in your arms with the strength of all your tenderness descend into the sea. All that animated you, all that moved you before, could move you forward in the world no longer. The water filled your mouth and your nostrils, and you choked at the taste of it. But when the grief or the guilt or the loss recedes into the night and your soul sets sail again, you still dream—despite yourself. There is still a kind of music you will hear that stirs within you an unspeakable longing. There is still an ache, not just for all you lost, but to see and know and be seen and known still, to explore and imagine and create. However much the longing for the past may assault your senses, it is not the only longing that remains. There is still a part of you that wants to make love, to feel yourself somehow connected. There is still a part of you that yearns for something outside yourself. You felt yourself out to sea, and yet some kind of desire, for something or another, bears you along, and you find yourself still somehow here—almost against your own wishes. And even in the moments when anything that felt like conscious desire went out with the tide, there is still some kind of near-morbid curiosity of how your life and story are going to turn out—even if you are lost enough to only behold what's left of your life as a kind of bystander.

Somewhere between your body's animal refusal to go down quietly, your mind's refusal to stop imagining, and your heart's refusal to stop dreaming, in the tangled mess of synapses and memories and impulses, there lies God. In whatever remains in you that wants to create, to make, to birth something new, in whatever corner that longs for some kind of resurrection on the other side of death, something divine quietly snaps, fires, clicks, flickers. This is the Spirit of God, lurking in your own broken spirit.

You may find that your grief and sense of loss over the world you once knew seem endless. And yet there are possibilities and potentialities within you that are more endless still. What is this unseen force that carries you forward despite yourself? Why can you not seem to choke, always and forever, your own irrational yearning, this buried but still breathing hope for more?

This ache is God's fingerprint. The stirring to create, to love, to live, to give of yourself when there is no self left to give—this comes from the Spirit. You were created in the image of God. Before you knew anyone or did anything, everything was in you necessary to live at home in divine love. However buried that image of God is within you, that part of you that knows what it is to be perfectly loved, held, and known—it is still very much there. There is a part of you that does not need anything else, or anyone else in particular, to be alive. There is a part of you that knows this—part of you that has *always* known this—but has long since forgotten.

The God who sustains all created things with love sustains you. The God who created the world not to be exploited, dominated, or needed, but to love and to enjoy without clinging, is awake in your belly. And so in you is the capacity to love and to live without needing the world to work out a certain way in order for you to be okay. Your life, your existence, is contingent on that Spirit. But it is not contingent on anyone else, or anything else.

> This ache is God's fingerprint. The stirring to create, to love, to live, to give of yourself when there is no self left to give—this comes from the Spirit.

This is the liberating, terrifying discovery of life on the other side of the shipwreck. That while you are a creature—humble, dependent, small, in need of love and food and shelter—you didn't need anything else as much as you thought you did. That the things you knew would kill you don't actually kill you. That the fire in you the sea should have drowned out, burns within you yet, if you do not let yourself smother it (and maybe even if you do). So much of the world you have known is no more. But if there is any truth in any of this at all, the shipwreck that threatened to destroy you utterly may be the thing that saves you yet. It may not drown you; it may transfigure you.

And if there is something truthful, something larger, about this irrational lust for life that is forged in the fires of death, it says something too about the people you lost. For if there is a God who not only creates but sustains and resurrects, then there can yet be life on the other side of death for all things. Then there is hope, not only for the yearning in you to drive you into union with God, but to be realized in union with those others. If death is not the final word, and chaos produces creation rather than destroys it, then many of the stories of the life you thought were long over are far from over yet.

Believing this won't mean you won't still feel the weight of deep, sharp, piercing grief, or that you should feel guilty when you do. On the contrary, people who don't experience deep pain have not experienced deep love and are not to be envied. That doesn't mean they are shallow—all of our souls surely have something of the same depths—they just may not be aware of their own yet. That day will come for them. But when you feel your own deep capacity for passion, compassion, mourning, even rage, you are glimpsing something of your soul's own infinite capacity to know, to feel, and to become. Within the depths of all you feel the most deeply, something of the Spirit's own immortal depths is reflected in you. We have a capacity for love and hope and beauty seemingly too big for our heads and hearts, because we are created in the image of God.

Cling to Nothing . . . but Hold On

After the shipwreck, when the ship is still going down and all you have left are bits of it still floating in the sea all around you, it's nearly impossible to tell at first what will actually hold you up. The ground that was once beneath your feet is now scattered all around you; and you know instinctively that much of what has gone before, you can't take with you now.

So the attempt to find something to hold you up is

often a very high-stakes kind of trial and error. Some of what was holding you up was built on lies, spin, and youthful delusions. You must let them float away. Some of the childish notions of how the world works—the illusion that you were ever truly in control of your life to begin with—you must let sink. Some of them made for a helpful enough vessel at the time, getting you from point *a* to point *b*, moving you forward. Some of the relationships that cannot and probably should not survive the storm served an invaluable function for a while. But the shipwreck has made new demands of your life, and much of what carried you before cannot carry you now—and you surely aren't in a position to carry much of anything with you now.

After the shipwreck, you may have little left to hold on to. And yet you must find a reason to hold on. This is much more difficult than it sounds, because surviving the shipwreck, in general, has much more to do with letting go than it does with holding on. You are now trying to simultaneously find a way to hold on while learning to live with open hands and an open heart—to not resist the wind, or the Spirit you find in it.

Growing up in Pentecostal churches, I spent a lot of my childhood attempting to chase down the Holy Ghost. The preacher would give an invitation for people to be filled with the Spirit—which we would know occurred when we let go of the ordered world of rational speech and God moved on us to talk with unknown tongues. Even where I parse some of these things differently now, there is still a way it makes some kind of soulish sense to me. Aren't we all, in some way or another, looking for an experience that will transcend the pale and paltry words we know? Isn't there something inside all of us that wants to howl, that wants to rumble, that wants to talk in unknown tongues? The letting go of mind and of ego, the sense of being acted upon by something larger, older, truer—surely there is something of this that the soul has always wanted, whether we can acknowledge it in our minds or with our words at all.

I remember going down to the altar, wanting the gift of the Spirit, but being confounded by the sweet old saints who tried to help me "pray through." I would be down at the front of the church, my eyes squeezed tightly shut and my hands raised like awkward lightning rods, praying to receive the power. And I'd have some dear old sister in one ear, shouting, *Hold on, brother!* And there would be some dear old sister in the other ear who would shout, *Let go, brother!* That is the Pentecostal version of paradox. I wasn't ready to explore many others, but that was one I got baptized into early. How is it possible to hold on and let go at the same time? I don't know that I can even answer that question now, but I do know life with God exists somewhere at that intersection. That somewhere between holding on and letting go is where you are liable to stumble into, or perhaps even collide into, resurrection. The old-time Pentecostals may have been even more right than they knew.

In the shipwreck, you find yourself smack-dab in the middle of having to let go of everything you thought you knew—and yet still trying to find a reason to hold on when you don't feel like you've got anything to hold on to.

One Small Plank

In the shipwreck, you may feel like you lost it all. Everything is in pieces. But in the fragments, there are planks that remain—pieces of desire, of dreams, of hope, of imagination, of longing, that rise to the top of you even now. They are no longer attached neatly together, but they are still afloat in the swirling chaos of you. You may not need all of them. Perhaps you don't need many of them. But you almost certainly need one of them. Wherever and however you feel your soul still adrift, grab hold of one of them. Don't cling too tightly to it; let the weight of it hold you up rather than the other way around. Anything that's survived by now surely has something of Spirit's power in it. It may be a plank that is older than you, a plank that might outlast you.

Grab something—anything—that will help you get through the night. That will help you make it to the shore.

It does not have to be anything big enough or strong enough to hold you up forever. Just something you can reach out for, lean your head against, and rest on when the night falls. Not enough to rebuild a life, but enough to get you to shore. You may think you will not yet survive the waves, but Spirit comes in the wind—to guide your giant soul and your tiny plank to a place called home.

You only need one small plank, one reason not to give up, one reason to stay alive . . . today. At the very least, your life itself is a sign and a sacrament for someone else, a light in someone else's darkness. There is not a thing in the world wrong with staying alive—for now—for their sake more than your own. That was what I found when I went to an Episcopal church in downtown Charlotte after I left the church—and it largely became that small plank for me. The simple liturgy, week after week, did not remove all my pain but gave me a reason to keep going—from one Sunday to the next Sunday, until the next, sustaining me somehow, then, in the days between.

It is always good and right in a time of shipwreck to cling to a community. It is good to cling to friends too, though part of what makes the shipwreck so intense is that by nature it's a time when friendships are largely being renegotiated. And of course, then, it is the best possible time to cling to God.

And yet even that does not come quite without qualification. It would seem this might be the easiest, most universal statement: "Well, at least you can still hold on to Jesus." The trouble with holding on to God is that often we cling to an old idea about God—perhaps one we needed to let go of all along—rather than to God himself.

Holding on to Jesus surely is always the right thing to do—unless you are Mary Magdalene, whom Jesus appears to first just after he rose from the dead. Her world has been eclipsed by the storm. Days before, she watched the man her heart burned for be tortured and killed. Now, the dead man is standing in front of her. Which is more disorienting? What is for certain is that her world is upended. Desperately, instinctively, she lunges for what is familiar— the body of Jesus impossibly standing in front of her now, only a few feet away. "Don't embrace me, Mary. I have not yet ascended to the Father," Jesus says.[2] It is not that

Jesus was no longer there for her; it is that Jesus cannot be there for her in the ways he was there for her before. She would have to come to know him in a different way. Resurrection had not yet finished working out its terrible implications. There would be no time to cling to a form of Jesus, an idea of Jesus, a vision of Jesus, she used to have. She would have to know him

> You can't even cling to the God you knew, *only to the God you can know now.*

now on the other side of the trauma that is resurrection, so that even "clinging to Jesus" was not going to work in the ways it had worked already.

You can't even cling to the God you knew, *only to the God you can know now.*

Let Go

So for Mary, as it is for most of us, the hardest part is not the holding on but the letting go. That was the part I really didn't know how to do. Because I never let go. I kept such a tight grasp on anything or anyone I claimed to love, and the more I hurt, the more I dug my fingernails into anything that would seem to keep me alive. I was so afraid of letting go.

One of the main reasons I could not let go was that I knew I was propping up other people. If I let go, what would happen to the people leaning on me? My heart was in tatters, but I stood there quivering, still clinging to the twin pillars of duty and obligation. I was not standing strong, but I was not lying down. When the storm first broke and I felt like I needed to quit, I remember the staff member who leaned in three times within fifteen minutes to say, "You cannot leave. *Livelihoods* are at stake." I was my father's son, the apple of his eye as a rising star in the denomination. What would my family do? And besides, this was a church I had helped bring into the world. What would the church do? I was trying to say, even though everything in me said my time was over, that the only hope for me was to pull the plug and put real weight down on the hope of resurrection. But I had convinced myself I could not, because too many people and too many things were dependent on me.

It is fascinating to me now to see how, even though I know better, there is something that feels pious and noble about that sentiment. That it sounds like God and gospel to me—to stay in at all costs because it is for someone else's sake. It is hard to hear the whisper of the ego underneath all that, saying, "You are *too important*."

Accepting Our Own Smallness

The primary obstacle to letting go is generally our own inflated opinions of ourselves—that our lives are too important, that too much depends on us . . . that the world cannot go on without us. Part of the function of the shipwreck is to show us the truth that was there long before the storm came: We are much smaller, and much less important, than we think we are.

While my world was imploding, I went by myself one Wednesday afternoon to see the film *All Is Lost*. I didn't go into a movie theater; I went into a metaphor. Everywhere I turned, there was language and images of sea—symbolic in Hebrew mythology of chaos, of the abyss. I knew no other way to describe the way I felt except lost at sea—adrift and alone. Which is of course precisely what the film is about. In it, seventy-seven-year-old Robert Redford plays a man whose boat is torn open at sea. His communications system is beyond repair.

The weathered Redford is by himself against the elements, a speck of a human against the unending mystery of the sea. There were two shots in that film that sliced through me. In one, the camera pans up slowly from the tiny raft he now occupied and just keeps going up, until the perspective crawls over you of just how small he is against the expanse of ocean. But there is a second shot I loved even more—essentially the same shot, but from the bottom of the raft. The camera descends lower and lower, slowly, until not only do you see the tiny raft from the opposite depth, but you also see a school of sharks swimming beneath him, undetected by the protagonist.

Months later, I was sitting downstairs in a tiny makeshift chapel on the bottom floor of a simple condo in San Diego, California. Across from me in the unadorned sanctuary was Sister Anne, a nun in her late sixties. There were no vestments, no ceremonial attire, just a simple black track jacket. She had a dark, natural tan in the easy way people do in Southern California, her face framed by short, soft white hair and gold-rimmed glasses. Her voice soothed the storm in me. Her eyes, bright and blue and young and curious, peered into the abyss that had swallowed me whole, unflinching. I knew little except there was no judgment in this tiny woman, that love seemed to follow her in like a song. For three days, she had been taking me apart, touching all my pressure points gently—I called her the Ignatian ninja. Each day, she sent me out into the place I most tended to avoid in the indoor sport that was my life—into the wild. Sometimes to the cliffs, sometimes to the pier, sometimes up a mountain. She said I needed to clear space for myself, that I needed to get to places where I could see and feel myself from God's point of view.

Sister Anne was also the extremely cultured nun who apparently sees all the credible new art films. She said to me, "Jonathan, I don't know if you have seen the film *All Is Lost* with Robert Redford. But it makes me think of you. It is about a man who had read all these books about the sea and had all these wonderful instruments. But it was not until he was an old man caught in a terrible storm that he finally had to learn how to use them for himself."

I could not help but laugh. Sister Anne was right. My knowledge was more theoretical than experiential. This was the season of on-the-job, in-the-storm training of the life-or-death variety. This was the divinity school with no roof, no bottom, no boundaries, and no end in sight.

I was a man out of his depth, dealing with the sea that had always been within me. But I never had the scale and perspective to see either my smallness or the infinite varieties of creatures that dwelled within my own depths. Of course I did not want to look at them.

I was not going to be able to let go as long as I thought the world was going to collapse if I did so. What I did know was that I thought I was going to have a nervous breakdown if I stayed where I was. As bad as I was at listening to my body or integrating it into my spirituality, I could not ignore it this time. So I gathered the pieces of myself that were left to be gathered and headed to that little Catholic retreat center in San Diego on just a few days' notice.

As I followed Sister Anne's instructions each day to go out into creation, she told me to feel the energy of the waves and water and wind—to let the Spirit blow through me and enter me through them. All week, I kept thinking about the verse in Acts where Paul says, "In him we live and move and have our being."[3] I would walk the cliffs and could not shake the awareness that the Spirit was actually in the wind. Never before in my life had I been so aware that when I did look at the rocks or the waves or the sky, God was in all of that, was holding all of it. Sometimes I would stop and lie down on the rocks, and I just couldn't escape the truth of it: "The Spirit is in the wind; the Spirit is in the wind; the Spirit is in the wind." The inescapability of God's love would not let me go:

> Where can I go from your spirit?
>> Or where can I flee from your presence?
> If I ascend to heaven, you are there;
>> if I make my bed in Sheol, you are there.
> If I take the wings of the morning
>> and settle at the farthest limits of the sea,
> even there your hand shall lead me,

and your right hand shall hold me fast.
If I say, "Surely the darkness shall cover me,
and the light around me become night,"
even the darkness is not dark to you;
the night is as bright as the day,
for darkness is as light to you.[4]

There is no escape from love. It fills all things. The Spirit of God—she fills all things. And I could feel her filling me, fractured and broken though I was.

It is an illusion-shattering thing to be outdoors, away from the insulation of rooms and hard corners, and face fully the essential wildness of things. In our own kingdoms of influence—our homes, our pulpits, our offices, our computers—we fancy ourselves in control, creators rather than conduits. Climate-controlled rooms delude us into thinking we can control God and the world. In reality, the thermostat is about all we can change. It's impossible to be people of the Spirit while disconnected from nature— the creation—where the Spirit's wildness can be learned. I needed to be away from the technology that says, "You are really *big*!" Nature says, "Oh honey, you are really, really small." We poke fun at ancient mythologies we find absurd while buying the most absurd of them all—the myth that we control things.

I was getting away from my delusions of control. I was getting back in touch with my own breath again. Sister Anne directed me to slow down my breathing, to breathe deeply, to let God set my breathing right again. In the evenings, I would go down to the little library at the center and wrap myself in a blanket, and imagine that the blanket was the love of God itself. Sitting in the little rocker, I would let myself be held. I would tell God how afraid I was.

"The conversion moment in us is when we see from a new perspective," Sister Anne said. "Sometimes all we can see is that this is not working for us anymore. That is all you can see, until you are ready to see from that new perspective." Everything she asked me to do that week was about perspective. To walk along the shore and pick up small rocks, allowing them to become stand-ins for all my troubles—and then fling them into the expanse of the ocean. As I did, I grasped their smallness; I heard the small plunk against the backdrop of the roar of the waves.

"God looks at us and sees us the way we see ants," Sister Anne told me one day. "We see them working so hard to build their little structures, and we think it is cute or even admirable. We enjoy their beauty for a moment. But we know the next day, someone will come along and step on their little ant colony, and all they worked so hard to build will be gone."

"God sees us as parents would see a two-year-old child," she continued. "They are sorry when they make a mess, but they are not surprised by it. They hate to see them hurt themselves in some way, but they are not angry at them for it. It is also true that our grandest successes, our biggest accomplishments, are like the drawings of a two-year-old. God delights in them only because he delights in us, but they are no more impressive. He just likes that we drew it. But they are still very small and simple to such a great God," she said. "That's how God sees your work," she added, smiling.

A shipwreck has a way of stripping you bare, of exposing your own finite smallness against the infinite horizon of a dark sea. Slowly but surely, I was being delivered from my own sense of importance. As I now know, it is possible to devote yourself to a life of piety, keep all the rules, and even engage in the spiritual disciplines—but leave the ego largely untouched. We have developed ways we can "be a good Christian" without ever embracing the descent into death and resurrection that would actually turn us into good human beings. I think a lot of this has to do with the project the church often sanctions every bit as much as the rest of the world does—the life of working hard to be a "success." In the words of Thomas Merton, "If I had a message to my contemporaries, I said, it was surely this: Be anything you like, be madmen, drunks, and bastards of every shape and form, but at all costs avoid one thing: success . . . If you are too obsessed with success, you will forget to live. If you have learned only how to be a success, your life has probably been wasted."[5]

The years prior to all this had been my most successful in ministry. And not just successful in the sense of climbing some ladder of temporal gain—it was the most effective preaching and teaching I had ever done. But there was so much of myself I had kept at bay. Sister Anne helped me see I was like the young surgeon she heard lecturing about suffering when she was in medical school (she was a very smart nun)—I knew all about the tools and instruments, but had not known about grief and pain before now, had not had to really wrestle with the mysteries for myself.

I don't think I had deeply come to know love yet either. In recent years, I had repeated revelations of the love of God, whether through Scripture, books, or things I would see in other people. But I had yet to really allow the love of God to settle over me in all my broken places, to come to really know divine love in the parts of me that seemed the most unlovable. My theory is that all of us elder sons of the church, the ones who spend all our lives trying to keep the rules, have a deep suspicion that if we do feel loved and accepted, it is because we are working so hard to get it right. Sister said it takes some people their whole lives to come to really believe God loves them. But that it had to be learned in a deep, experiential way—as it is the key to existence. She said that no matter how long it took, God is relentlessly determined for me to really *know* this for myself. Sister Anne said the whole trauma I was experiencing—of going through hell, of falling apart, of death and resurrection—was for my good, so I could really know.

Per usual, God did not answer any of the questions I went to San Diego asking—questions about ministry and marriage, about what would come next. But I did feel like God spoke to me, again in that way when you feel things inside you shift, and it is as if some new word has been planted in the topsoil of you—small and green and hopeful. I tried to pray a lot that week, often in its most primal forms of letting my very breath become prayer. Mindful, attentive, at peace for the first time in five months, I would stand on the pier at night and watch the waves roll in and out, knowing they were coming in and out long before I got there, and they would continue to long after I was gone. Walking through a graveyard on a mountain, I tasted my smallness in a world where so many people are being born and are dying—and do so with or without me. Looking out over the ocean, I saw my smallness against the horizon.

The search for meaning is a quest for power we are not designed to bear, an obstacle to the grace of insignificance. What could prepare us for the breath of God (Spirit) that hums all life into being, except we be emptied of our pretensions of significance? Divine perspective most of all relativizes our importance. We are each very small creatures. Very little is contingent on us. Knowing our smallness puts us in touch with the essential lightness of created things—transitory, ephemeral creatures. Splendid irrelevance. All lives are small lives; all epic struggles are skirmishes, because we are weightless creations, deceived by an illusory sense of gravity. Inside the movie inside our head, we all feel like we are stars. It's an illusion. We're all extras.

> Destinies do not rest on our shoulders. We are given choices, but the cosmos runs with or without us. And that is all grace.

The gospel doesn't fulfill our quest for significance, but exposes its essential folly. It gives us something better than meaning—namely, love. The love of God gives us unfathomable value despite our objective smallness. But it still leaves us blissfully unimportant.

The two central exchanges in my own time with God, as best as I could discern them, went something like this:

Me: "God, I can't take this. I honestly think I'm falling apart."

God: "What would be so wrong with you falling apart?"

Me: "Well . . . I mean, I've got this thing you gave me to do. And I don't think I can do it anymore. I think I'm going to have to go sell french fries at McDonald's."

God: "Who told you you couldn't work at McDonald's?"

I was starting to see. I am a creature: made, dependent, small. I know less than I think I do. I think more rides on my existence than it ever does. I was coming to see that wisdom is not having the right answers but having a proper sense of scale and perspective. Wisdom is embracing our blissful smallness. If we think the world needs us too much, we can't receive life as gift. And if we can't receive life as a gift, we can't receive it at all. The tides keep coming in and out; the flowers keep growing; people keep being born and dying. It all keeps running, not contingent on us.

Destinies do not rest on our shoulders. We are given choices, but the cosmos runs with or without us. And that is all grace.

Chapter Four

Eating, Breathing, Sleeping

*Out of the darkness of my life, so much
frustrated, I put before you the one great thing
to love on earth: the Blessed Sacrament . . . There
you will find romance, glory, honour, fidelity,
and the true way of all your loves upon earth.*

J. R. R. Tolkien

*Holy Communion is offered to all, as surely as
the living Jesus Christ is for all, as surely as all of
us are not divided in him, but belong together as
brothers and sisters, all of us poor sinners, all of
us rich through his mercy. Amen.*

Karl Barth

Perhaps the most universal experience in any and all
kinds of shipwrecks is the way they strip us down to
the primary colors of being human. There are so many
things we have, that we come to think we need, that we
feel we cannot live without. On the one hand, the prospect
of liberation that the shipwreck offers (if we survive it!) is

a life where we are set free from that illusory sense of need for things that are not necessary at all. In the shipwreck, we come to find out the list of things we need to stay alive is relatively short—we need to breathe, we need to eat, we need to sleep, we need companionship of some kind. A shipwreck is the most radical act of cleaning out our closets. When we get over the initial terror of it, there is a kind of exhilaration in getting rid of so much we never really needed but thought we could not live without. It is good to not feel ourselves so dependent on things that never really sustained us to begin with. Through the horror of our losses, we slowly gain a clarity, composure, and clearheadedness that was never available to us before the storm.

What makes this so complex, however, is that in the same moment we are finding these essentials are all we really need to survive—breathing, eating, sleeping, friendship—we also find ourselves struggling with these most basic human practices we may have taken for granted before. We did not worry too much about having enough oxygen, until we were plunged into the depths of the sea. We didn't worry too much about dinner, when we knew there would be plenty of money to go out for it. We didn't think too hard about sleeping, before the shipwreck invaded our dreams and disrupted our sleep. We discover we had all the essential things we needed to survive in us and around us all along, while at the exact same time we are discovering these things are now harder to come by than they ever were before.

Whereas the early stages of shipwreck entail a sense of panic, a frantic kind of triage, trying to figure out what we can salvage and what we cannot, eventually we have to slow down . . . and return to those primary colors. In order to not drown, we have to find a way to ground our bodies long enough to figure out how to breathe and sleep and be again, without the comfort and props we had before. It is not easy to do, because nothing is easy to do after the shipwreck. But the gift is a kind of simplicity: I don't have time or strength enough now to wrestle with large existential questions. I cannot fix anybody else's problems. I am not strong enough to be productive in all the ways I was before. I have to stay alive. I have to survive. So I have to figure out a way to do all of these things, again . . . somehow.

The apostle Paul is one of the master teachers in any and all wisdom traditions, a man you would want to talk to in order to find answers to all your questions about finding meaning in the cosmos. And yet in our Acts 27 story, when Paul receives revelation by the Spirit that he and his companions were about to experience a shipwreck, Paul does not give them philosophical, theological, abstract counsel. All too often, people of faith like me behave more like the friends of Job than the friends of Jesus, lecturing, pontificating, preaching, or explaining suffering—well-intentioned maybe, but useless in the face of real pain. But the apostle is wise enough not to say anything smart or clever, wowing his boat mates with penetrating insights into the meaning of the sea and the existential function of the shipwreck. Instead, Paul gives them astonishingly bald, unadorned, practical advice that will help keep them alive:

"For the last fourteen days," he said, "you have been in constant suspense and have gone without food—you haven't eaten anything. Now I urge you to take some food. You need it to survive. Not one of you will lose a single hair from his head." After he said this, he took some bread and gave thanks to God in front of them all. Then he broke it and began to eat. They were all encouraged and ate some food themselves. Altogether there were 276 of us on board. When they had eaten as much as they wanted, they lightened the ship by throwing the grain into the sea.[1]

Paul says in effect, "You've worried yourselves to death, so much so that you haven't even been able to eat. You'll be okay, but only if you eat enough so the storm doesn't take too much out of you when it hits." As it is with all hungry and hurting people, they didn't need a philosophy seminar; they needed to be fed. They didn't need meaning; they needed a meal. Paul was an expert Jewish teacher, but he doesn't break down Torah law for the sailors; he breaks bread for them. He gives thanks; then he distributes the bread. This fits the pattern of how God responds to human suffering: We come looking for answers; God sends a hot meal through a warm body. We come looking for reasons for our hunger; God sends provision to feed us. We come looking for a sermon that will explain the complexity of the cosmos to us and satiate our

> People try to offer us an explanation; God offers us a Eucharist.

desire for understanding; Christ responds with, "This is my body, given for you; this is my blood, shed for you."

People try to offer us an explanation; God offers us a Eucharist.

Eating

The meal Paul offers may be called "a Eucharist" for a handful of reasons. Eucharist, by definition, is "giving thanks." It's a meal Paul gives thanks for, blesses, and distributes to everyone on board, regardless of tribe or tradition. I presume that Luke, the author of Acts, knows what he is doing in using language and imagery so rich in eucharistic imagery, connecting it with the ritual as established in the earliest Christian communities. And I do believe there is something consecrated, something remarkably other, about this meal in particular, which I'll return to shortly.

But for our purposes here, it's important to put the eucharistic meal in the context of the broader story of God and humanity. At least part of the reason God reveals himself in flesh and blood in Jesus of Nazareth, the incarnate Word made flesh, is to show us that all humans are holy. The gospels place a relentless emphasis on the bodily resurrection of Jesus, because it is through attending to the sacredness of his earthly body that we can learn to recognize the sacredness of all bodies. We recognize sacred spaces and consecrate holy ground, because it is in these places that we can learn to live in the reality that all space is sacred and all ground is holy because God created and sustains it. In the same way, part of the function of the holy meal, the Eucharist, is that through this consecrated supper, we are learning to recognize the essential holiness of all suppers. Even the honor given to the priest or pastor who presides over the meal is teaching us, if we are paying attention, to regard all those who will ever prepare a meal for us as holy chefs. In the consecration of the elements, we see that all who cook and prepare bread and wine for the sake of caring for someone else's body reenact the liturgy. If we are wise, perhaps we may learn to bow to all of them yet.

When we are able to eat on the other side of a shipwreck, all meals are especially holy, because the sea and storm have sapped us of all our former strength. The primal blessing of food, so often taken for granted, is exotic to us again. How is it, anyway, that no matter how much or how badly we have suffered, even when it does entail not wanting to eat for a few days, we still get hungry again, and that against all odds, food tastes good to us still? Isn't it fascinating that even when we are completely out of sorts, there is something about a meal (any meal), that grounds us again in our humanity—especially when it's a meal shared with others?

When you are trying to survive a shipwreck, I am very much in favor of eating. I will not put parameters on this. I am sure that when you are dealing with physical or psychological trauma, there are many benefits to eating clean and healthy so your body can function as well as possible. I would not argue against this. There have been times of shipwreck when a very disciplined diet, the routine of monitoring what I ate when, seemed to have a soothing quality, providing a kind of order and stability in times when the world was all chaos. I would celebrate anything that helps you survive a storm, including embracing the mental and physical sharpness that comes with reducing carbs and sugars—though I love them more than I love you and would choose their survival in the event of apocalypse over your own.

But short of recommending alcoholism or cocaine, I'm a pretty big fan of the whatever-it-takes-to-get-you-through-the-night diet as well. Maybe you shouldn't have cheesecake every night forever, but if you'd look forward to it, be fully present to it, and be grateful for it, let the cheesecake tether you again to what is good about the earth. Let the cheesecake make you believe in God again, and the idea that there must still be something good left on earth because of how good this is tasting right now. Whatever meal would make you feel like giving thanks is provision that syncs you again to the Provider. If it's between eating something you love and hating your life tonight, eat something good—and make no apology for it! And if you need to be healthy to keep your strength up to survive the shipwreck over the long haul, eat the cheesecake tonight, and an apple in the morning—and start over. Now is not the best time to agonize over the calorie count. To eat is to be human, to eat is to celebrate being alive—especially when you eat with other people. If there is a place you can go to be fed a meal, and a person you know with whom you can enjoy a meal, this is no small part of what it takes to survive a shipwreck.

Those small moments of gratitude may be the only thing that keeps you afloat. It is not selfish to do what you have to do to take care of yourself in the wake of all the pain. Nights will come when the taste of food may be the closest thing to feeling anything at all, and that is okay. A hot meal can tether you to reality again, root you down in the provision of God. For a moment, it can make you feel human, and when there is nothing else you know how to feel grateful for, it may just be reason enough to mutter "thanks" under your breath—and be aware, if even for a moment, this meal means you are not entirely alone.

But there is a special place for the consecrated meal in the season of shipwreck too. I do not come from a tradition where we partook of Communion often, at least in my corner of the tradition. But during my years as a pastor, the power of this practice came alive in my life and the life of our church in such a transformative way. We celebrated weekly Communion at the church, and the idea that Jesus was tangibly present in the celebration of this meal became our dominant narrative—though that is historically uncommon in a North American Pentecostal church. But at the church, I was always the one in the position of serving, not of being served. In a way I cannot entirely explain even now, one of the first things that shifted in me when my shipwreck happened was a desperate hunger for the tangible, tasteable presence of God through the experience of the Eucharist—now needing to be carried to the table, now needing to be served rather than to serve.

After I left the church I founded, I was so hungry to encounter God through the Lord's Supper. In my own journey, my belief in the real presence of Christ in the Eucharist had long become the center of my faith. I was aching to find a place where I could receive the body and blood of Jesus every single week. So I shuffled into the big red doors of St. Peter's in uptown Charlotte a little awkwardly, a self-proclaimed hillbilly Pentecostal. The aesthetics of the place were foreign to me. Yet in a way, the simple artistry of the space made room for a sense of wonder, reverence, and otherness that made me feel at home in a place I did not precisely know but had longed for. I don't remember how long it took for me not to cry all the way through every service. I could close my eyes when the choir was singing behind us and actually feel like angels were singing over me. For all the ways some people may think of Episcopal churches in North America as rest homes for progressive white people, I can only tell you that St. Peter's is as ethnically diverse a church as I've been in. From the African-American male rector and white female associate rector, to the revolving door of beautiful faces in the pews around me, the church seems as integrated socioeconomically and culturally as it does ethnically.

I loved the warmth and compassion that seemed to radiate off the walls in there, and I loved being stone-cold anonymous. Off the grid from my evangelical circles, I felt completely safe to come as I was—to receive, to just be. I loved that it never felt like the church was trying to sell me anything. I loved that, really, nobody is fussed over at all—there just is not that kind of VIP treatment for anybody. The vibe is, "This is the kind of worship we do here, and you are welcome to come and do this with us . . . or not." The liturgy there does not try to coerce everyone into the same emotional experience, but in its corporate unity strangely creates space for us all to have a very personal experience of God. I have commented to friends that I have never actually prayed this much in church before.

With my own world feeling disordered and untethered, I was quite happy to be told when to kneel and when to sit and when to stand. I love that there was almost no space in the worship experience to spectate, because almost every moment invites (but not demands) participation. I had been in no position to tell my heart what to do. But because the church told my body what to do in worship, my heart was able to follow—sometimes. And that was enough.

It never felt like a tragedy there to not be the guy up front speaking—I'd been preaching since I was nineteen years old. That part is only gift. Ironically, as long-winded of a preacher as I was, I loved investing in a way of being and doing church where preaching really isn't all that central to begin with. In the Anglican tradition, preaching is never the main event. Preaching is only foreplay at most. All the weight of the liturgy lands on the Eucharist— preparing for it, receiving it, reflecting on it. I loved being part of a worship experience where so much emphasis is placed on the broken body and shed blood of Christ. I loved that I get to come and actually kneel at the altar, where someone looks me in the eye (when I hold my head up high enough for them to do so) and gives the elements to me. I cry around that altar week after week. When my heart is too overwhelmed, I slip out the side door after I receive the Eucharist, where a sweet older man and woman lay their hands on me and pray for me. After years of being in healing lines down at the front of the church waiting for evangelists to lay hands on me, I surely don't feel any shame or self-consciousness about just sliding into that back room for prayer. I go as often as I need to, without reservation. All this love and beauty, and they give the body and blood of Jesus away for free every week to anybody who wants it.

This Daily Bread

None of this helped me figure out, with any degree of clarity, where my life was headed. The prayer Jesus gave us to pray is, "Give us this day our daily bread."[2] There is no prayer for future bread. Like the manna God provided in the exodus story, there is bread that is supplied day by day, that cannot be kept or stored for the days ahead. It can only be received on this day, and then we will have to ask all over again the next day—learning to be dependent, at home in our creatureliness.

The word *this* is our only defense against the guilt of the past and the anxiety of the future. *This* daily bread. *This* chair you are sitting in. *This* song on the radio. *This* person sitting beside you now. *This* meal you are about to eat. We can't go back into the past and fix any old moments or propel ourselves into the future to find whatever is lurking there. All we can do is open our hands and our hearts to receive the gift of this meal, this day, this friend, this moment. *This* daily bread tethers us to the provision we have in this moment, however small—the only moment we have. "This" anchors us to the ground when we are floating, at least for a few fleeting seconds.

We need something more immediate than a memory of how God was revealed in the past, more immediate than mere hope that God will be revealed in the future. God can only be known and experienced in this moment—right here, right now. If we will attend to this moment, God will attend to us.

> If we will attend to this moment, God will attend to us.

Trying to find a way to attend to the moment myself, in that season where every step in every direction felt excruciating, I wrote this prayer as a way of tethering myself to the grace of this moment. I hope it can help you find the grace in whatever moment you're in right now:

> *I do not ask*
> *for some future bread.*
> *I do not ask*
> *for some lofty thing.*
> *I ask for nothing more,*
> *I ask for nothing less,*
> *than primal provision.*
> *For this, and this—only this.*
> *I do not ask for then.*
> *I do not ask for there.*
> *I do not ask for that.*
> *Only this meal—this moment.*

For this day, only
for this, and this—only this.

Holy Breath

Before my own shipwreck, I can't even recall a time when I ever really paid attention to my breathing. Which is, in a manner of speaking, a way of saying I wasn't paying attention to my life. It seems so clear now—how primal the connection is between Spirit and breath. No wonder in Hebrew and in Greek, the words for *spirit* and *breath* are the same. God is not just the source of breath; God *is* our breath—the Spirit fills our lungs even now, making each moment possible. "In him we live and move and have our being," Paul writes,[3] and this is one of the primary ways that God actively sustains all living things—through the gift of divine breath (is there any other kind?). Whatever kind of sea we may be swimming in (or drowning in), we are all somehow contained in the ocean of God himself, the source of all our being. If there is no other evidence in your life that God loves you, is there for you, or provides for you, consider the evidence of your own breath—each inhale and each exhale carrying with it the message that God is choosing you all over again, now, in this moment . . . in this breath.

And yet when the body is under duress, as I experienced often in my own shipwreck, it can feel like oxygen is in short supply. The very air that fills us with life, with possibility, with Spirit, is more difficult to access through labored, heavy breathing or short gasps of air. Returning to our breath is a way of returning to reality, the deeper reality than the crisis of our identity as creatures sustained by a God of love. Returning to our breath, being attentive to it, receiving the gift of it, is a primal way of returning to God himself. Do not let anyone ever convince you that only people with a certain spiritual pedigree have access to the Spirit. You know the Spirit is available to you, because of your constant access to the holy breath she gives you.

I was not connected to any such essential realities until the shipwreck made me feel like I was constantly on the verge of going under, and air did in fact feel in short supply. It is a long and wonderful story how a self-proclaimed hillbilly Pentecostal ended up flat on his back in a yoga studio, wearing an eye mask, lying under a blanket, smelling incense in the air—while my new friend James played a drum in the background. I mean, I once would have been suspicious of people who used incense in church! But driven by desperation, there I was, with a kind of tribal music playing in the background.

James is a Christian, though his breathing class is not explicitly Christian in its approach. He does talk about the connection between breath and spirit, how God fills us with holy breath, and how we can follow that breath where it leads us. I was so far broken open at that point, and my life felt so unmanageable—I was open to get to God anyhow, anyway, those days. Even if that meant a man in a tank top playing a drum was going to have to teach me how to breathe all over again. (I can't even imagine how much some of my friends reading this are going to want to travel back in time to stage an intervention.) But I felt astonishingly safe. So when all the pent-up grief in me came out, I didn't just cry; I wailed. I lost all track of myself. I'm glad they play the music loud, but then again, I was probably too far past myself to care what anybody else would have said. Every ounce of grief, of guilt, came out in what felt like an eternal kind of travail. And yet I felt so completely loved, somehow beheld so tenderly by the presence of Love himself. It was not Love in the abstract, but Love in the particular, the God revealed in Jesus of Nazareth, which is the only God I know. And how this God did meet me in that space. The deeper in I went, the more immersed I felt in the love of God. I had never experienced anything like it before.

I knew in my head that "in him we live and move and have our being."[4] I remembered Sister Anne, when I was on spiritual retreat, asking me to be mindful of God at work, holding together the dirt and rocks and sand and sky all around me when I walked the cliffs. But I don't think I ever *knew* experientially before that moment that God is not just a being; God is being itself. I don't think I ever really knew experientially the way David described God in the Psalms: "If I make my bed in the depths, you are there. If I rise on the wings of the dawn, if I settle on the far side of the sea, even there your hand will guide me, your right hand will hold me fast."[5] I don't think I ever really comprehended that this God literally could not be outrun, no matter where I fled or what I did. The very fact I exist means I exist in God and am sustained by God, literally with every single breath. The inescapable presence is the only reason I am able to be . . . anywhere, anytime, at all.

In case I have not made this sound sufficiently strange, I've had a consistent image in my mind the last few minutes of the new puppy my parents had bought—Gabi. While staying at their house—a thirty-six-year-old man feeling like a complete loser—them getting that sweet little dog had helped keep me alive. She didn't judge anything about my life or my heart. She just loved to see me come home to this place that was not my home, and she just wanted to be with me and play. The love of God was being manifested in the face of a dog that never takes her eyes off me, never wants me to leave, and always wants to draw me into life, laughter, and the wonder of the present moment.

I cried. Then I laughed. Then I cried-laughed, and laughed-cried. It was the experience I always wanted to find in the Pentecostal altar services. And to be clear, I believe in all of that, and I think there was in fact an encounter with the Spirit to be had in those places. It wasn't God who wasn't ready, but me. Before I was broken open by my own suffering, my own pain, even the pain I caused, I couldn't have dropped far enough from my head into my heart and body to enter fully into such a moment. Only in the experience of feeling bankrupt in every conceivable way—an absurd man living an absurd alternate version of my own life—did I reach the point of seeing I had no choice but to let go. How could there be any holding off that Presence now, when I couldn't even hold myself together?

I'm near delirious on the love of God, lying on the mat in a yoga studio, in an environment where there are no explicit markers of Christian worship at all. I had been lost in all the ways I never wanted, and thus finally in a posture where I could get lost in all the ways I always did want, but couldn't. James does little to direct the experience—he lets the Spirit work through us in the breathing. But a few moments later, I felt like God revealed to me an aspect of my life I was carrying in a way that was positively crushing me, consuming me . . . killing me. While it was deep, quiet, and entirely interior in the way I understand the voice of God to most often be, it was perhaps as clear as I felt I had ever heard the Spirit inside me. Echoing in the deepest chambers of my being, I heard these simple words: "You don't have to carry it anymore." Almost as soon as the phrase formed inside me, James bent down and gently whispered in my ear, out loud: "You don't have to carry it anymore, my brother."

Toward the end of the session, James bent down one more time and gently laid his hand on me. He was close enough to my head to where I could hear his voice softly above the music behind us.

He was speaking in tongues.

You certainly would not have to attend a class, like I did with James, to welcome in the presence of God through the holy breath you are taking right at this moment. The presence is available in the air all around you, waiting for you to pay attention, waiting for you to wake up to love. But part of the value of the experience for me is in the same way the consecrated meal of the Eucharist helps me recognize the fundamental ways that all meals are holy. The consecrated, set-aside space for breathing helped me become attentive to the Spirit available in all of our breathing.

When we breathe—slowly, intentionally, mindful of the

source of life that fills our lungs now—we return to who we really are. The sights and sounds of the world around us now in its clutter and clamor, of life in the city—and even the sensory assault of a life that now feels under water—all recede, and we return to the garden. The Holy One communes with us still, creates us still, sustains us still, breathes in us still. Being attentive in just one breath—being open to the Spirit in just one breath—is to open ourselves up to the source of all life and the source of all healing. The Spirit comes to us, riding on our own breath, summoning us back home into the quiet, gentle care of the One who keeps us alive moment by moment, filling our lungs.

Sleeping

I have less to say about this than eating or breathing, because in a way, sleeping is the simplest of these elemental blessings that call us back to life and to the source of life in a shipwreck. We are constantly overwhelmed with new data that tells us how many physiological and psychological benefits there are to sleeping, and how many risks there are associated with the lack of it. And yet, I'm quite sure most of us know this intuitively. The problem is not that we do not recognize our need for sleep or don't have a proper scientific understanding of its benefits, but that we just aren't actually sleeping. And during a time of shipwreck, there are so many, many reasons not to sleep.

Shipwrecked nights are the longest and slowest of nights. There is endless time to sit with your longing, your hurt, your desire, your despair, or your grief; there is endless time to replay what you did wrong and what you wish you had done differently. The loneliness, the isolation of the night—the sense of being caged inside your own skin—is profound. There are so many monsters, which we will look at later, that come out in the night.

I think often of the story of Elijah the prophet, who is on the run from people who want to kill him, now tired and hungry, and convinced he's the last man God has to stand for him on the earth. Paranoid and exhausted, he finally falls asleep—he literally takes a nap. And when he wakes up—look here! God supplied a biscuit. Oh, and wait—there are actually seven thousand other prophets he didn't know about! The food mattered. The knowledge that he was objectively not alone made a difference. But none of it was possible until he went to sleep. The world was not going to get any less threatening and he was not going to feel any more hopeful as long as he was sleep deprived.

When the shipwreck takes its toll on your body and your mind and you are utterly overwhelmed, sometimes you have to bravely pull the covers over your head and sleep it off. If you are sleeping fourteen hours a day and can't get up in the mornings, and you are depressed, someone can help you with that too—and there is never any shame in getting help to survive a shipwreck. It is essential. But I find most often in times of shipwreck, people suffer more from lack of sleep than from sleeping too much. The season is so long and so demanding that you get so used to living frantic, harried, panicked—there is no time for sleep. There is too much to worry about, too much to figure out!

There is no better medicine for the syndrome scientifically known as "God-doesn't-love-me-everyone-hates-me-I-just-want-to-die" than sleep. Sleep, in its own way, is an act of trust. We enter into the realm of the unconscious—vulnerable, where we cannot think, work, or wrangle. Even the most devout atheist enters into this act of surrender, this letting go into the night that lets us go into God as the one who sustains us, who keeps watch while we are no longer looking at our watches. And with or without our cooperation, when we sleep, God is at work to heal and restore what has been lost in the day's eternal battle with the sea. We take leave of the world we know to enter a world we do not know as well, and we are held. Frederick Buechner writes these words:

> Whether you're just or unjust, you have the innocence of a cat dozing under the stove. Whether you're old or young, homely or fair, you take on the serenity of marble. You have given up being in charge of your life. You have put yourself into the hands of the night.
>
> It is a rehearsal for the final laying down of arms, of course, when you trust yourself to the same unseen benevolence to see you through the dark and to wake you when the time comes—with new hope, new strength—into the return again of light.[6]

More pertinently, when sea and shipwreck have almost taken you under, "life is grace. Sleep is forgiveness. The night absolves. Darkness wipes the slate clean, not spotless to be sure, but clean enough for another day's chalking."[7]

I am not a doctor. But I am fairly convinced that anything from warm baths to special teas to boring fiction to Ambien is supremely better than not sleeping. If even in this moment, you are feeling so overwhelmed by the savage nature of your own life at sea, may I recommend that you not sit here long enough to ponder how you feel about the value of sleep as some sort of idea? This is one of the most tried and true ways to let God in—through a small and necessary act of letting go. If you can sleep now, even for a little while, you may well wake up to find a new set of glasses on the nightstand through which you might see the world and the storm outside in an entirely different way.

I know—you don't have much time, and you have other things to do. Set your clock if you absolutely must. But in this moment, God is waiting for you under the clock of your own slumber. Put the book down, and everything else you are carrying.

Sleep now. Trust now. Brother, sister, you don't have to carry it anymore.

Not tonight.

Chapter Five

God Loves Monsters

If only we would let ourselves be dominated
as things do by some immense storm,
we would become strong too, and not need names.
When we win it's with small things,
and the triumph itself makes us small.
What is extraordinary and eternal
does not want to be bent by us . . .
Winning does not tempt that man.
This is how he grows: by being beaten, decisively,
by constantly greater beings.

Rainer Maria Rilke

There's something important here I need to tell you. On the other side of the shipwreck, you will make an ominous discovery: You are not alone out here in the water.

Like that brilliant shot in *All Is Lost*, there are sharks swimming beneath the waters of a shipwreck. You aren't going to make it all the way to shore without running into some monsters, without staring them down, without naming them. Whatever storm, whatever crisis, may have caused the shipwreck may not be nearly as scary as the things you have to confront while floating out here, on the other side of where your ship sunk. When we are shipwrecked, everything that has lurked beneath the surface of our lives will rise from the bottom to meet us—and these are not beautiful creatures. Everything we've tried to push down for so long—every flaw and fault we've denied or ignored, every truth we'd rather not come to terms with—all of this will come to light in the crisis of a shipwreck.

And we're not going to make it safely to shore unless we deal with these monsters we've not dealt with for so long.

In pop culture, we have a lot of make-believe monsters. Let's put them aside for a minute. The real-world creatures that most stir the imagination of great writers and film-makers, even when we make up monsters from outer space, are the ones that actually live under the water. No wonder director James Cameron, famous for science-fiction films like *Aliens* and *Avatar*, made a documentary on deep-sea life called *Aliens of the Deep*. It is the closest thing to our imagination of aliens in outer space we have ever found.

After the devastating tsunami that swept through the Indian Ocean in 2004, all sorts of freakish-looking sea creatures were captured on film and in photos. These really were the sort of beings we have only envisioned in fanta-sies about life on Mars. But these were not the product of Hollywood special effects. All of our strangest and most beautiful exotic life-forms live deep beneath the surface— and God knows how many human beings have yet to see them. Some are so deep into the shadows that they may never be discovered.

In antiquity, images of dragons were drawn on the

far end of sea maps. The places off the edge of the world we knew were where the sea monsters lived. People have always been afraid of what creatures may lurk in the deep, which is why so many of us choose lives where we stay on the surface of things. Then the monsters we repress are the ones that control us. Because nothing in the world is as powerful as the things we're afraid of. What we are afraid of, we bury deepest in our big souls, to lurk in our shadows with room enough to grow into dragons and space enough to rule us with terror. Whatever we fear, we empower.

Repressing that which lives in the chaos beneath us is a perfectly good way to live an ordered life, but not a way to live a full one. We cannot and should not simply always do what we feel, but on some level, we can only do what we truly want—at least if we want to live as whole, integrated people. We have to come to terms with the desires that live in the depths of us, and not just ignore them. The monsters can't be eliminated—only tamed (by something beyond ourselves) and integrated—somehow including them honestly in our awakened, above-the-surface lives instead of pushing them to the bottom of things as if they don't exist. When we attempt to live as if the sea monsters do not exist, the dive into the depths is a dive into uncharted waters. Yet to not acknowledge the truth of their existence is to ignore the truth of ourselves, which is the greatest form of deception. Counterintuitively, the monsters are most likely to eat us if we attempt to ignore them. Simply put, sea monsters need loving too.

Early in my life, I established a pattern—anything in me that I was afraid of, any desire that overwhelmed me, any passion that scared me, I pushed in the darkness. I was nearly incapable of looking at anything in me that seemed unpleasant. I pushed down any part of me that was sexual, competitive, proud, or otherwise unseemly. I did not fight the dragons; I ignored them—which is another way of saying that I fed them. I lived as if I was without a shadow side. But when the life you knew crashes against the rocks, everything in you comes crawling out. That's when you discover the things about yourself you've long ignored or repressed. And you are able to truly behold them face-to-face instead of through the murky veil of self-delusion and positive spin. You can see now, without the filter of your own inner PR firm. The monsters you heard rumors of are firm with reality now; they objectively exist not just within you but now somehow objectively outside of you. In the moonlight on the night you broke open, the evidence is staring back at you with fierce, black eyes. Hello, terrible, beautiful, wild true self . . . it's nice to meet you.

Leviathan, God's Rubber Ducky

There are monsters in the depths of the ocean—this bears out in every credible witness in antiquity. There are monsters in the depths of us—this bears out in every credible witness in psychology. Any religion that fails to take into account the reality of sea monsters should never be taken seriously. Thankfully, ancient Judaism takes sea monsters quite seriously indeed. There are many references throughout the Old Testament to the ancient sea monster,

Leviathan. Some have contended these descriptions were intended to attest to the existence of alligators, but I find that unlikely. Leviathan in the ancient world generally had a mythic quality, like our Loch Ness monster.

My favorite description of God in the Scriptures involves this mythic being. In Psalm 104.24–26, God is celebrated in this way:

> Any religion that fails to take into account the reality of sea monsters should never be taken seriously.

> O LORD, how manifold are your works!
>> In wisdom you have made them all;
>> the earth is full of your creatures.
> Yonder is the sea, great and wide,
>> creeping things innumerable are there,
>> living things both small and great.
> There go the ships,
>> and Leviathan that you formed to sport in it.

I'm not sure which is more fascinating here—the depiction of Leviathan or the depiction of God. We are talking about the mysterious, primordial sea creature that terrorized the depths. Leviathan represented everything about the world that is disordered, disorienting, and frightening to human sensibilities. In a word, Leviathan represented chaos—the primal forces at work in the cosmos that we cannot know or understand, much less domesticate or control.

We can imagine the dominant role such a being played in the consciousness of an ancient seaman, a strange being that summed up the volatile nature of the sea itself—unfathomably large, powerful, and utterly indifferent to human expectations or demands. Leviathan, then, has a long and prestigious history in world literature. When Herman Melville wrote *Moby Dick*, the awful, terrifying descriptions of the fearsome whale are peppered with biblical allusions to Leviathan. The whale seems to somehow personify this ancient terror.

And yet in the psalmist's powerful imagination, this being is for God a household pet. If God were *Sesame Street*'s Ernie, the sea is his bathtub, and Leviathan his rubber ducky. People say our choice in pets says something about us, whether or not you are a dog person, a cat person, a bird person—whatever. But what exactly does it say about God that he has the chaos monster for his pet?

As we will see, God likes to talk a lot about Leviathan—or at least the Hebrew poets who wrote words to us on God's behalf like to do so. When I was in my own shipwreck, if I have ever received any kind of real revelation from Scripture, it was on Leviathan, the sea monster. The task now is to translate this somehow in a way that does not feel remotely academic or clinical. Because in many ways, what I believed God showed me about monsters became a lifeline for me. If I had continued on my normal course of denying the existence of the ugly truth within, I would still be living a half-life. But instead of renouncing the monsters I held inside myself, I had to learn to swim with them.

Confronting the Monster in Me

Growing up in the church, I always found a way to feel guilty, even when I had nothing of substance to feel guilty about. I was prone to long bouts of figuratively beating myself up, paralyzed by even the smallest of missteps. I was terrified of hurting God or someone around me and finding myself somehow outside the purview of grace. After my shipwreck, for the first time, there really was plenty I felt guilty about, and I felt suffocated by the shame. I could not look in the mirror without seeing the black of accusation and mistrust in my own eyes.

Those voices were largely internal then. But finally, a moment came when someone else articulated externally all the things I said about myself inwardly. It was one of the worst moments of my shipwreck, and also one of the most important.

It happened soon after I left the church and my marriage disintegrated further. Separated then, I was getting ready to leave my house after being at home for the weekend. I had just gotten done giving our little dog a bath. And then, from upstairs, I saw a truck speeding into my driveway going more than fifty miles an hour. It belonged to a man who had been very important in my life and who felt a great deal of hurt and anger about the way things had gone downhill in my marriage. I hurried down the stairs, but before I even got to the bottom of the stairs, he burst through my back door and was standing at the bottom of the stairwell, confronting me. This man, then and now, I believe to be a deeply good man. But he had his own issues to work through, just like I did—and he had come over in a fit of blind rage.

Having lived so much of my life as the world's most overgrown boy scout, relatively drama free, the whole thing felt like something out of a film of someone else's life, not a scene from my own.

He had a lot of choice words for me about what I was and what I was not, and about my father, and about how he was going to show me what a real man was—"since you didn't grow up with one in your house." Nothing about that moment defined who this person was or is to me, any more than my worst moments did for me. But as he ordered me to sit down—threatening my life, telling me what I was going to do and not do, storming around my living room—the horror scene became even more bizarre. It was as if he was reading from a script that contained every fear I ever harbored, with frightening particularity. "I hope you know there is no forgiveness for men like you!" he said. "You've already blasphemed the Holy Spirit. You've already *stomped the nails of the cross so far into Jesus* [as he stomped his foot wildly]. There is no going back for men like you. You think now you can just pray some little prayer for forgiveness? There is no forgiveness for men like you. You've already crossed the line. You're lost forever!" Line by line, it was everything in my life I had ever been afraid of, back when I lived every day in fear I had committed the unpardonable sin. But now I was already buried under my own sense of guilt and responsibility; I already felt like I had let down everyone I loved in walking away from my church, and I already felt incapable of repairing any of the things I felt like I had broken—myself included.

I kept calm and steady, did not raise my voice, and did not even speak, except when this man I cared for asked me to repeat back to him, screaming in my face, "Do you *understand me*, boy?" In which case, I responded, "Yes, I understand you." I knew then that what I confronted that night was not this well-intentioned, otherwise peaceful man at all. I was confronting something much more ancient and more primal, something that knew all the words I was most afraid of and was able to quote them to me, chapter and verse.

In many ways, I was staring down my own monster within for the first time in my life—all the accusations, all the fears that had most driven my true self underground all of those years.

It was one of the most traumatic moments in my life—but also one of the most important. When I would not engage this man's rage by matching outburst for outburst, he finally gave up, stomped out, and sped away. And while my nerves were jangled, in an odd way, I had never felt calmer. I knew—as an absolute matter of fact—that nothing that was just said to me was true. I had plenty of moments of feeling monstrous. I was no longer appealing to any of my old merit badges. I knew deep down that I was not a monster at all. What I was, what I am . . . is a failure. A deeply flawed, deeply loved human being with a great capacity for good and a great capacity for evil, just like everyone else.

My faith did not fail, even when I did. I did not lose

my soul, even when I lost my ship. Even if I was, in fact, a monster, the God I love is the God who loves monsters and knows how to tame them.

Given time, this man regretted his actions deeply, and by God's grace, we were able to reconcile. I have no bitterness about this violent encounter, and if anything, I'm only grateful it afforded the opportunity to stare down my own demons. It was the worst kind of confrontation imaginable for me, the thing I had on some level always been most afraid of. But in the face of all the monsters—from my wayward heart to his monstrous rage—love stared down them all, and love won.

Braving the Deep

While I did not believe God labeled me a monster, I was in fact coming to terms with all the things that were monstrous within. If my knowledge of the monsters was theoretical before, it could not be anymore. I was having to name them, one by one—behold them, confront them, surrender them all to God.

Each of us have monsters that live in our depths. Like all mythological sea monsters, they are too big and too powerful to be caged. The mysteries we attempt to cage are the ones most likely to eat us. We can first only invite God into our depths, knowing he is more comfortable in these depths than we are, and begin to see these creatures through his light. We cannot be captivated by a murderous desire to destroy them. Attempting to eradicate them is both futile and dangerous. This is the blasphemous plight of Captain Ahab in Herman Melville's *Moby Dick*—he is obsessed with conquering and killing the mystery, a pursuit always tantamount to madness. We cannot kill the monsters, only behold them in ways we once refused to, and allow them to be exposed before the only One with the credentials to handle them. Killing monsters is above your pay grade, no matter who you are.

I had read the Bible all my life and desperately needed some guide to help me name the monsters. During the time I was on sabbatical from the church, I spent hours in a little condo alone, digging in ancient texts, and I found an unlikely map in the book of Job, one of the most enigmatic and poetically gorgeous portions of Scripture. It is not a place I would have previously thought to look, because Job is famously a tale about a blameless man. We are rarely blameless, and in my case, I had never been more cognizant of just how nonblameless I really was. I had blamed myself for various global crises most of my life—crises of the "I didn't share my faith with this person who was going to become a missionary and therefore entire tribes did not hear the gospel" variety. You can also see how large an ego there was in me to deconstruct, even if it was a self-flagellating one. Those really are monstrous! So now how was I going to manage actual blame rather than the artificial kind I had always been so proficient at generating within myself?

Thankfully, blamelessness is not necessary for Job to come to life within us. In fact, there is nothing particularly moralistic about this ancient poem, at least not as we have come to think of such things. Job is the book of the Bible perhaps most chock-full of all the big mysteries, of all the deep questions. It is the book most articulate in teaching us how to wrestle (or in some cases again just reverently behold) the monsters that come from the deep.

Here are the basic contours of the story: Job is the book that introduces the idea of a satan to us.[1] Later traditions will collapse different images into a patchwork theology of this figure, including the serpent in the garden of Eden, for example. But of course, Genesis never comes close to using language of "satan" or a "devil," and so the identity of the serpent is shadowy at best. Even in Job, this satan is not introduced with some kind of personal name (though most translations follow tradition and use an abbreviated title, Satan), much less a backstory. The personification of evil in Job is rendered in the Hebrew as *hassatan*—"the satan." He occupies an office rather than being, say, a guy named Satan. The word simply means "the accuser." This figure is literally the embodiment of accusation. And if Job's account is taken seriously, accusation is not just what this figure does, but who he is. Accusation is as intrinsic to what this being is as love is intrinsic to who God is. In the Hebrew imagination, accusation is the very essence of evil.

The accuser—the prosecuting attorney—comes to the courts of heaven doing his job—filing accusations. But in this case, he accuses God's seeming pet human, Job. The accusation is a simple one: The satan says this being does not have a "disinterested" love for God. In other words, he does not love God on his own terms; he only loves God because God had made him healthy, wealthy, and wise.

Take all these things away from him, the accuser says, and this man you love so much will curse you.

Through the epic poetry of the book of Job, we see the trial take place. Job is afflicted beyond measure. Within days, he loses his children, his land, his livestock, his health. Everything about his external world is shattered. The figure of the satan is not mentioned again in the book—as is typical in Hebrew theology, there is not a great deal of speculation or interest in how evil may be personified. He exits early, but this diabolical prosecutor is not needed to carry out the case against Job. He is not needed, because Job's friends do such an excellent job of taking care of it for him.

Here Job is, the portrait of a man undone, and all he wants now is the consolation and empathy of his friends. But Job's friends are precisely the kind of friends we often are if we have not suffered—they are more interested in explaining Job's plight to him than sitting with him in it. They are incapable of the compassion that would demand them to suffer with Job, to suffer alongside him. They cannot do this, because Job's story had become a threat to them. These were law-abiding Jobs who did everything within their power to be upright according to the law. And the popular understanding of the law—even seemingly underwritten in, say, a book like Proverbs—is that as long as you do the right thing, good things will happen to you as a reward for your obedience. Only the wicked suffer, and it is because of their misdeeds.

So when they speak their long, in the Job character's phrase, "windy words," it is less a commentary on Job's plight than it is on their own.[2] These were men who, like so many of us, desperately needed the world to be ordered. And if the world did not operate according to a system of merit, then the chaos could touch them too. And that was unthinkable. Rather than entertaining the possibility that the kind of terror that befell Job could ever come on them too, they do what all religious communities do when their sense of order and control is somehow threatened—they label the monster and cast him out. And for these men, the monster is unequivocally Job.

This is what we do when we do not understand someone else's story. Their story disrupts our sense of order, so we have no choice but to accuse and blame them. Accusation has no place in any sort of authentic spirituality. Accusation is always an attempt to expel a threat by turning another human being into a monster. As René Girard puts it, Job was the "victim of his people," the victim of the system of sacrifice and scapegoating that is almost universal both in mythology and in history.[3] If we look to Job's own words, the labeling and rejection he experienced from his religious community were even more painful to him than all he actually lost! People want a sense of order and control, and they will gladly turn someone else into a monster in order to have it.

It is the antithesis to everything Jesus taught and demonstrated through his very life. The cross of Jesus, in the torture of the only truly innocent man who has ever lived, exposed the sham of human violence and accusation. Jesus came not as the accuser who hurls stones at us for our sin but as the advocate for humanity. He is not the defense attorney for the not guilty, as there are none who are not guilty—all are complicit in the rejection of God. Jesus is the one who says, "Father, forgive them; for they do not know what they are doing,"[4] even while he hung on the cross, the one who "while we still were sinners . . . died for us," in the words of Saint Paul.[5]

Unlike Job, I have been far from blameless in my life. But I am like Job in this respect: Even while he refuted the charges against him, he began to internalize the names hurled at him. He began to think perhaps he really was a monster. So often when we see something in us that frightens us, we think we are monstrous—and thus not loved by God.

The God Who Celebrates the Chaos Monster

If Job was, in fact, a monster, he assumed he was on the wrong side of God. Like his friends, he lived in a world where people thought of God as the karma police, the one who enforces "what goes around comes around." So he presumed God's job was to kill the monsters. He presumed God and monsters have an adversarial relationship. Early on in his complaint, he decides to let the feelings in the depths of him go free in the form of his words:

> "Therefore I will not restrain my mouth;
>> I will speak in the anguish of my spirit;
>> I will complain in the bitterness of my soul.
> Am I the Sea, or the Dragon,
>> that you set a guard over me?"[6]

Note the movement: Job sees his own inarticulate feelings as the monster. Finally he decides he will not restrain these monstrous feelings any longer. So he calls out to God, "Am I the Sea, or the Dragon, that you set a guard over me?" Do you see what lies behind Job's petition here? He thinks it is God's job to serve as Leviathan's parole officer. He thinks God is the one who keeps Leviathan from getting off his leash and roaming free.

Job believes God is the one who crushes the monsters. So now that his life has gone all to pieces, he believes himself to be the monster. How could not God also crush him?

> If I summoned him and he answered me,
>> I do not believe that he would listen to my
>> voice.
> For he crushes me with a tempest,
>> and multiplies my wounds without cause;
> he will not let me get my breath,
>> but fills me with bitterness.
> If it is a contest of strength,
>> he is the strong one!
> If it is a matter of justice,
>> who can summon him?[7]

For Job, God is the one who uses the storm and the sea to crush the monsters. He is the one who will not let me get my breath. If we have a showdown, how could I ever overpower the dragon slayer?

God is the one who . . .

By his power he stilled the Sea;
> by his understanding he struck down Rahab
> ["monster of the sea and purveyor of
> chaos"[8]].

By his wind the heavens were made fair;
> his hand pierced the fleeing serpent.[9]

He stills the sea where the sea monster lives; he pierces the bizarre creatures as they slither away from him. Job, though, unlike most of us, has the courage to continue to stare into the abyss long enough until a voice calls out to him from the whirlwind. He stares into the storm until he finally finds the gaze staring back at him. The storm addresses him by name. The speeches of God are short in the book of Job compared to the speeches of Job and his friends—another way we see the wisdom of Job, for in real life we proportionally do a lot more of the talking than God does.

But God finally does speak. When he does, he doesn't offer Job any explanations. Instead, he does a rather shocking thing: He begins to talk to Job about Leviathan, the sea monster. He begins by teasing Job, who has been pontificating for so long, asking him whether or not Job was there when he actually shut in the doors to the sea of chaos and put boundaries around it—if Job was there when he put a boundary around the waves. And that's when he really goes after it, celebrating the sea monster:

"Can you draw out Leviathan with a fishhook,
> or press down its tongue with a cord?

Can you put a rope in its nose,
> or pierce its jaw with a hook? . . .
Lay hands on it;
> think of the battle; you will not do it again!
Any hope of capturing it will be disappointed;
> were not even the gods overwhelmed at the
> > sight of it?
No one is so fierce as to dare to stir it up.
> Who can stand before it?
Who can confront it and be safe?
> —under the whole heaven, who?"[10]

Then God launches into a description of Leviathan's mighty powers, boasting of its thunderous limbs, its "double coat of mail" like that of a dragon,[11] and its terror-inciting teeth. When Leviathan opens its mouth, God says, "sparks of fire leap out."[12]

God compares Leviathan's sneezes to lightning flashing in the sky, his breath to the kindling of coal, and any weapons set against it as useless as straw.[13] Clearly, this is not a beast to mess with.

"When it raises itself up the gods are afraid;
> at the crashing they are beside themselves.
Though the sword reaches it, it does not avail,
> nor does the spear, the dart, or the javelin . . .
It makes the deep boil like a pot;
> it makes the sea like a pot of ointment.
It leaves a shining wake behind it;
> one would think the deep to be white-haired.

On earth it has no equal,
a creature without fear.
It surveys everything that is lofty;
it is king over all that are proud."[14]

God's speech is incredible, yet its tone is more playful than harsh. "Tell me, Job. Could you bring Leviathan home as a pet for your girls? Could you have Leviathan whisper sweet nothings in your ear?" And of course the right answer is *no*. But the implicit idea is that *God absolutely could* do those things. God is at home in the chaos—it is the place from which he started the universe. God is at home with the chaos monster. The monster does not threaten or intimidate God. For us to attempt to subdue and defeat Leviathan somehow would be madness, just as it was for Herman Melville's Ahab to think he could kill Moby Dick.

The monster was not a threat to God. And while Job had become a threat to his friends, he wasn't a threat to God either. The creature the world called "monster," God called "friend." The beautiful part, then, is that the people the world calls "monster" (because their appearance, their story, their otherness feels monstrous to those around them) are the ones God calls "friend." All the things that made Leviathan so frightening to everyone else were what made Leviathan delightful to God. God celebrated all the wild things about Leviathan that made everyone else recoil in horror.

In fact, in an especially strange turn of the poem, in some translations God not only celebrates Leviathan but also identifies with Leviathan. Watch how God seems to casually move between how people respond to Leviathan and how they actually respond to him:

> "See! Any expectation of it will be disappointed.
>> One is overwhelmed even at the sight of it.
> There is no one fierce enough to rouse it.
>> Who can take a stand before me?
> Who will confront me? I will repay him!
>> Under all the heavens, it is mine."[15]

God is at home with the wildness in Leviathan, because Leviathan is a product of the wildness in God. In the account of creation, we read, "So God created the great sea monsters and every living creature that moves."[16] Leviathan is not a dragon for God to slay, but a pet that reflects the unpredictability of its creator. As Timothy Beal writes, here we see "a spectacle not of a God who sits enthroned over chaos, not of a God who subdues chaos, but of a God who rouses it, who stirs it up, who revels in it."[17]

Bringing Leviathan into the Light

What if, then, God does not have the adversarial relationship with the monsters we once assumed he had? God is not scandalized, shocked, or frightened by anything within us. Properly speaking, the monsters are not nearly as dangerous to us as our fear of them—a fear that pushes us into hiding from the safety of God and community.

Do you feel like you are monstrous? The good news is
that God loves monsters. God is the only one who can tame
them. A full frontal assault on the monsters, à la Captain
Ahab, is only going to rile them up and put us in over
our heads in a battle we cannot
win, with flimsy harpoons in our
hands. Since there is nothing we
can do to tame the monster, our
only recourse is to welcome God
into the depths that are his natural habitat, inviting the beautiful
Spirit back into the place where
she has always belonged.

> The monsters are not
> nearly as dangerous to
> us as our fear of them—a
> fear that pushes us into
> hiding from the safety
> of God and community.

"Even the darkness is not dark to you," the ancient
king David writes.[18] In the New Testament, the apostle
John writes, "If we walk in the light as he himself is in the
light, we have fellowship with one another, and the blood
of Jesus his Son cleanses us from all sin."[19] The ultimate
sin in that first Johannine letter is to "claim to be without
sin."[20] Walking in holiness is not to walk in perfection but
to walk in authenticity, to walk in truth. That does not
mean we will not have any broken pieces. That does not
mean everything within us will yet become well and whole.
But the first and largest step toward wholeness is always
to invite the light of God into our depths, and to invite a
few friends along who we can trust to hold the light for us
when needed (preferably not friends like Job's).

What we absolutely cannot do is attempt to wage a
quiet war against Leviathan. That is inevitably going to be

an unwinnable war against our very selves—a war that will cost us our health, our sanity, our well-being. It is a life of quiet desperation.

I am too young and inexperienced in this business of inviting God into my depths to be an expert on any of this. I do not think there is a one-size-fits-all answer as to how God will deal with the monsters within. What I do know is that all true desire has its origin in God and can open us up to God. Even if the desire gets misplaced or misappropriated, even if we attempt to fulfill the desire where it cannot be fulfilled, the desire itself, the primal energy, originates in God himself. Even the chaotic ones.

If there is any hope to harness the monsters' power, to put a hook through their noses, to do something constructive or hopeful with them—that is far above our very limited capacities. We cannot expect to master them, but only to open them up to light and air, where God and others can help us to see them with a sense of scale and perspective. When we come to glimpse something of the transcendent love of God, that is when we realize we have nothing to fear from the monsters anymore. Because there is nothing in the universe that can outrun God's love, nothing that will not get smaller underneath the heat of his burning affection.

I wish I could have known this earlier in my life, because I think there could have been less traumatic ways of dealing with my own monsters. But I'm grateful for the God I've come to know from navigating the waters of my own chaos. He doesn't orchestrate the chaos to teach us a lesson. We don't live in a tightly ordered universe where

God is moving us around in an intergalactic game of chess. Rather we live in a world where somehow—far beyond our own limited capacity to understand the world or the way it works—God is always working to bring something beautiful in and through the chaos.

The Descent of Grace

But that is not the only thing I learned through my immersion in the world of Job, my immersion into the sea with the sea monsters. Walking around assuming God was angry with me, and that I could thus only expect dreadful things in whatever life I might eke out on the other side of the abyss, I figured I was marked. I concluded I was cursed for getting on the wrong side of this God. I was in so many ways still living in that primitive world of retribution, that sad land yet to be enchanted by grace. In the new world I was going to have to now inhabit, I was dead in the water if I tried to live by the religion of Job's "friends."

One of the things that makes the book of Job so profound is that it shatters the world of merit and demerit altogether. It is the book in the Old Testament that most clearly paves the way for how Jesus describes God his Father in the New Testament as the one who "makes his sun rise on the evil and on the good, and sends rain on the just and on the unjust."[21] Gustavo Gutiérrez writes these brilliant words in his book *On Job*:

Inspired by the experience of his own innocence, Job bitterly criticized the theology of temporal retribution as maintained in his day and expounded by his friends. And he was right to do so. But his challenge stopped halfway and, as a result, except at moments when his deep faith and trust in God broke through, he could not escape the dilemma so cogently presented by his friends: if he was innocent, then God was guilty. God subsequently rebuked Job for remaining prisoner of this either-or mentality (see 40:8). What he should have done was to leap the fence set up around him by this sclerotic theology that is so dangerously close to idolatry, run free in the fields of God's love, and breathe an unrestricted air like the animals described in God's argument—animals that humans cannot domesticate. The world outside the fence is the world of gratuitousness; it is there that God dwells and there that God's friends find a joyous welcome . . . The Lord is not prisoner of the "give to me and I will give to you" mentality. Nothing, no human work however valuable, merits grace, for if it did, grace would cease to be grace. This is the heart of the message of the book of Job.[22]

There is no escaping the fact that we will have to deal at times with the intrinsic consequences of our own actions—I have learned that all too well. But God is not the one who enforces the laws of gravity, of cause and effect, as some sort of extra punishment. God is the one who interrupts that natural cycle with grace. He is the one who, in the words of Gutiérrez, enables us to "run free in the fields of God's love, and breathe an unrestricted air like the animals." No matter what reasons we seem to have to fear ourselves or our monsters, God is decisively *not* the one we have to be afraid of. He brings the grace that can engineer beauty out of our chaos. He opens up new possibilities beyond simply living out the consequences of our choices. That may be part of our story, but it need not be the whole story—not in a universe where a God like that exists.

For if God is the one who brings creation out of chaos and turns chaos monsters into house pets, what do we ultimately have to be afraid of? It does not mean we will not experience, or be the cause of, deep brokenness in the world. It does mean there are no dead ends. We can behold the world in its beauty and ugliness without fear, and we can behold ourselves—as well as our monsters—without fear. "Here is the world," Frederick Buechner writes. "Beautiful and terrible things will happen. Don't be afraid."[23]

> It is love's nature to plumb the depths— of the earth, of our lives, of ourselves. It spirals downward into the very core of us.

The message of Job is not just that "bad things happen to good people." In a world of chaos, that is often the case. But the broader revelation is that none of us get what we deserve. There is grace and beauty extended to us all, even in the depths of whatever hell we might be currently occupying. The love of God, like the Son of God, who, in the words of the Apostles' Creed, "descended into hell," is always bent downward. It is love's nature to plumb the depths—of the earth, of our lives, of ourselves. It spirals downward into the very core of us.

In his story titled "The Dead," James Joyce depicts the reality of grace more poignantly and more beautifully than I have ever read anywhere else. It is the kind of beauty that haunts you, the kind of beauty that could only originate in God. It is the world that God makes possible, and that Job makes possible, for you and for me, for the guilty as well as for the innocent:

> A few light taps upon the pane made him turn to the window. It had begun to snow again. He watched sleepily the flakes, silver and dark, falling obliquely against the lamplight. The time had come for him to set out on his journey westward. Yes, the newspapers were right: snow was general all over Ireland. It was falling on every part of the dark central plain, on the treeless hills, falling softly upon the Bog of Allen and, farther westward, softly falling into the dark mutinous Shannon waves. It was falling, too, upon every part of the lonely churchyard on the hill where Michael Furey lay buried. It lay thickly drifted on the crooked crosses and headstones, on the spears of the little gate, on the barren thorns. His soul swooned slowly as he heard the snow falling faintly through the universe and faintly falling, like the descent of their last end, upon all the living and the dead.[24]

Of course grace falls faintly. It descends on everything and everyone, no matter who we are or where we come from. What else could grace do but descend, like the snow and the Son of Love who created it?

Perhaps even on the monsters. Perhaps even on me.

Chapter Six

Choose Your Own Adventure

Kiss a lover,
Dance a measure,
Find your name
And buried treasure.
Face your life,
It's pain,
It's pleasure,
Leave no path untaken.

Neil Gaiman

Once we have accepted our own smallness in the face of the shipwreck, embraced the humiliation of receiving help from others, and begun to come to terms with the monsters that live within—and the ferocious grace that God offers us in all this—we can begin to live from a deeper place. Deep living comes out of deep healing, which requires us to go deeply into our pain, mistakes, and failures to find the God who meets us there at the bottom. This is the slow, painful process of soul work. But as we do go further into the process, a whole new way of living is made available to us. Where we once simply ignored all that is in the depths of us, duty and obligation were often the only things that kept us afloat. But staying afloat is not the same thing as living from our depths. When we are not living from the depths, we are not living from our souls—we aren't living out of our deepest desires. Oftentimes, we develop an entire religion out of a system of "shoulds" and "oughts." At our earliest stages of development, this is no big deal. It's a classic exchange between parents and children—"Why can't I do that?" "Because I said so!"

But we aren't built to live in this stage for long. If we do not deal with what lives in our depths, we will live as fragmented, repressed, and often secretly angry people. This is why bad religion often turns out to be more toxic for people than no religion. We cannot live our lives with no sense of order or boundaries. But to replace a life without boundaries with a slavish system of "shoulds" and "oughts" will actually leave us worse off than we were before. That is a religion based on fear. This is exactly what Jesus describes in his rebuke of the religious leaders of his day: "Woe to you, scribes and Pharisees, hypocrites! For you cross sea and land to make a single convert, and you make the new convert twice as much a child of hell as yourselves."[1]

This is why it's so heartbreaking when people feel like they are forced or coerced into knowing and loving God— "you must love God or else!" In the very act of saying *you must*, we virtually ensure the person will never feel like they actually choose God for themselves. When we do not feel we have a choice, we cannot truly make one. We are

cut off from living out of our depths, and thus cut off ultimately from ourselves.

Before shipwreck, many people don't have a sense they
have actually chosen their own lives. When I was a kid, I
loved the "choose your own adventure" books, my favorite
of which were all G.I. Joe-related. The choices you made
in the book determined the story, so you could send in
the infantry—or the ninjas—and then turn to page 85 or
page 132 to find out your fate. Sometimes your G.I. Joe
squad lived, and sometimes they died, depending on how
you chose, but the thrill of being part of the story and not
a mere slave to arbitrary outcomes was exhilarating to me
then, and really is as much now. If God is writing a book
out of the stories of our lives at
all, I'm convinced this is how he
is writing it.

> Because we are designed
> to make choices, whole-
> ness is not possible as
> long as the life we live
> is not the life we have
> chosen, all the way
> down to the bottom.

Because we are designed to
make choices, wholeness is not
possible as long as the life we live
is not the life we have chosen, all
the way down to the bottom. This
does not mean we have to love
or even like everything about our lives, or that we can't
choose to make decisions out of a sense of sacrifice. But
even so, we have to know what we are sacrificing and why.
Our life is not entirely our life until it becomes the life
we've chosen.

The Biggest Obstacle to Living Out of Our Depths

The biggest obstacle to living out of our depths, I've found, is our own fear.

When I was a kid, I spent my summer days at my dear Pentecostal grandmother's house. Those were magical times for me. She was a sweet, Southern grandmother who made Tang and fried cornbread for me every day. We would sit on the couch and watch *The Price Is Right* and play Scrabble. My grandmother was a woman who deeply loved me and deeply loved Jesus. I still feel like a lot of the most important things I've learned about God, I learned from her, though she's been gone for eighteen years.

I remember one morning in particular when the cable went out. She called the company, and they sent out a repairman. When the friendly cable guy knocked on the door, a thought seized me. I had been hearing so much about how I needed to tell people about Jesus. *I am supposed to witness to this man*, I thought. And then the terror came. I was eight years old. How am I going to share my faith with an adult man?

I was suddenly paralyzed. I was terrified to talk to him, but even more terrified to not talk to him—because I did not want to be held responsible for his eternal soul. If I didn't witness to him, then he would not hear the gospel. And he could get in a car wreck on his way to his next job and would have to go to hell for eternity. And because he didn't hear the gospel, he would not become the missionary he was supposed to become. Which would mean some kid in tribal Africa would not hear the gospel because he did not hear the gospel, and I would be responsible for an entire village going to hell! After agonizing deliberation, I walked into the living room awkwardly where he was trying to work, and I asked him a handful of questions about his life. But I could not muster up the courage to ask him if he knew Jesus as his personal Lord and Savior. I just couldn't do it.

So when he left, I burst into tears. My grandmother came into the living room and asked me what was wrong. I could barely answer her through my tears. Finally I sputtered out, using words from the prophet Ezekiel, "I didn't share the Lord with the cable repair man—and now I know his blood is going to be on my hands!" It was pretty intense for an eight-year-old, but that is how I lived every moment of my life—always afraid of Jesus coming over the horizon at any second to call me to account for my sins. My grandmother was, as always, tender and wise. "Oh, Jonathan, that's not how God works! The way I see it, when I get an opportunity to tell someone the good things the Lord has done in my life, it's always a blessing. And when I don't do it, sometimes I feel like I miss out on the blessing of telling my testimony. But that is all—God isn't mad at you for not sharing your testimony with the cable repairman."

But that was the system I internalized, and that is how I always interpreted anything I thought God might be calling me to do. It wasn't an invitation, but a threat. I grew up feeling sure God was holding a gun to my head, saying "do this or else." Everything I did for God, even when I grew much older, was still done out of a sense of duty and obligation. No wonder I was so stuck in my head. When you are living in constant fear, there is no way you can choose to live out of your depths.

Perfect Love Casts Out Fear

God does not want us to choose life with him—or anything else about our lives—out of fear. "Perfect love casts out fear," the apostle John writes.[2] God wants us to choose life with him—and everything else about our lives—out of the safety of knowing how deeply we are loved, not because we are terrified of potential consequences of disappointing him.

Elizabeth Lesser illustrates this idea powerfully in the context of the relationship between human parents and their sons and daughters in her book *Broken Open*. She writes about reading Margaret Wise Brown's famous children's book, *The Runaway Bunny*, to her two sons. The sweet little tale begins like this: "Once there was a little bunny who wanted to run away. So he said to his mother, 'I am running away.' 'If you run away,' said his mother, 'I will run after you. For you are my little bunny.'"[3] So from there, the little bunny keeps coming up with wild schemes to get away from his mother. But no matter where he chooses to go or what he chooses to become, his mother changes into whatever she needs to be to get back to him. One of Elizabeth Lesser's sons loved the book and was comforted by the image of the mother who would not let her little bunny get away, no matter what. But her son Daniel didn't like it.

He was frustrated that the little bunny could not make his escape and would cheer for him to actually get away from the mother, shouting, "Run away, bunny!"[4] He would even come up with new schemes of his own for the little bunny to use that might actually enable him to get away.

This doesn't sound super masculine for me to admit, but the truth is that I've always had a thing about bunnies. I love them. I think bunnies are somehow kind of superfluously beautiful. They always make me think of grace. They have kind of been my totem. At different times and places in my life, I will see a bunny and be reminded in just the right moment of God's beauty and faithfulness to me. So when I read that passage in Lesser's book, it deeply resonated with me. I felt like a runaway bunny who could not find his way back home. I loved the image of God pursuing me at all costs, going wherever he had to go and becoming whatever he had to become in order to get to me. It made me think of David's psalm: "If I take the wings of the morning and settle at the farthest limits of the sea, even there your hand shall lead me, and your right hand shall hold me fast."[5] And indeed I do think there is a beautiful picture of God in *The Runaway Bunny*. I do believe there is a way the love of God pursues us, no matter where we go, a love that will not leave us alone. I am humbled by that love and grateful for that love.

But alas, that was not the central message *Broken Open* had for me. Feeling the tender wound of my own heart, I kept reading. Lesser came to realize that as her sons grew up, their process of individuation meant they had to have seasons of distance from their mother. Today she is extremely close to her sons. But she does not believe this would be possible now if she had not been willing to grant them the necessary space to make their own choices. She ends that section in her book this way:

> If you find yourself holding tight to your children long past appropriateness or helpfulness, perhaps it would help if you took down an old copy of *The Runaway Bunny*. Sit on the couch next to your stunned son or daughter, and read the book aloud. Only this time, change the words. Read it like this: *Once there was a little bunny who wanted to run away. So he said to his mother, "I am running away." "If you run away," said his mother, "I will let you go. For you are grown now. I trust you to find your way in the world. Run away, bunny!"*[6]

When I finished reading that section, I was stunned. I just assumed the message I needed to hear—since it's one I've so often struggled to internalize, was the message of God's everlasting, relentless, unconditional love. And in a way it was, but not in the way I presumed. God loved me enough to not hold the gun to my head and tell me what I should or must do from here. God loved me enough not to say, "Do this or else." God loved me enough to say, "Now you are at a place in your life where you are going to have to make some choices of your own." God did not want me to live in the shallows of duty and obligation anymore. It was time to learn to live from my true self—to learn to live out of my depths. And there would be no way to do that without the love that grants us freedom.

Choosing One's Self

I wish I could spare you the pain of having to learn anything the hard way. But the fact is, moments of getting life very wrong are often necessary if we are to become people who can choose their own lives. There is no way to come to know the stark truth about ourselves—or the beautiful truth of a loving God—without going straight through the passage of failure.

In many ways, this is embedded in the story of Scripture from the very beginning. In Genesis, when God tells Adam and Eve they can eat from any tree in the garden except for the tree of the knowledge of good and evil, the fruit glistens with inevitability. How could they choose anything else? In order for them to live awake, for them to become fully human, they will have to make their own choice—even the wrong choice. Strangely enough, it is only in making the wrong choice that they will be able to return to their native state of dependence again—to need the God who loves, saves, and restores. Partaking of the fruit is a necessary part of the universal human journey.

The Catholic psychologist Rollo May articulated this brilliantly in *Man's Search for Himself.* For May, the goal of human development is that we all, in Kierkegaard's phrase, come to ultimately "choose one's self."[7] There is no way this can happen unless we are given a real choice:

> It is doubtful whether anyone really begins to live, that is, to affirm and choose his own existence, until he has frankly confronted the terrifying fact that he could wipe

out his existence but chooses not to. Since one is free to die, he is free also to live. The mass patterns of routine are broken; he no longer exists as an accidental result of his parents having conceived him, of his growing up and living as an infinitesimal item on the treadmill of cause and effect, marrying, begetting new children, growing old and dying. Since he could have chosen to die but chose not to, every act thereafter has to some extent been made possible because of that choice. Every act then has its special element of freedom.[8]

This is why moralistic religion actually becomes dangerous for us, how it makes us "twice as much a child of hell" as a Pharisee.[9] As May demonstrates, those who have been taught that happiness and success will follow their "being good"—and who understand being good merely as a kind of external obedience—are not able to develop their own ethical awareness and strength: "By being obedient to external requirements over a long period of time, he loses his real powers of ethical, responsible choice. Strange as it sounds, then, the powers of these people to achieve goodness and the joy which goes with it are diminished."[10]

May sees many problems in human society as results of a culture where people do not have the rites of passage that enable them to really take responsibility for their own lives. When people continue to live out of duty and obligation, keeping the rules only so that others will tell them they are good, they end up with contempt for themselves. Living dependent on the approval of others means we never develop our own sense of dignity and self-esteem—really, our own sense of self. May puts it this way:

> Vanity and narcissism—the compulsive needs to be admired and praised—undermine one's own courage, for one then fights on someone else's conviction rather than one's own . . .
>
> When one acts to gain someone else's praise, furthermore, the act itself is a living reminder of the feeling of weakness and worthlessness: otherwise there would be no need to prostitute one's attitudes. This often leads to the "cowardly" feeling which is the most bitter humiliation of all—the humiliation of having co-operated knowingly in one's own vanquishment.[11]

It was by no means a happy discovery to see that at thirty-six, I had not, in very fundamental ways, really grown up yet. I was being plunged into the depths of my own soul and my own life, and the sea was raging. I would have given anything to make the churning stop. And yet the more I came to see the necessity of this phase of the journey—even though it seemed to mean my complete unraveling—the more I started to experience peace. Sometimes being thrown into the ocean is God's way not of abandoning us but of saving us.

Love Leaves the Door Open

Love does not lock us in. Love always leaves the door open. If we don't feel like we have a choice, then we are never able to really make any of our own choices. I used to live so much of my life afraid God would punish me for doing the wrong thing. But what I've come to learn is that the consequences of our actions are intrinsic—it is very true that "the wages of sin is death."[12] There is never any real danger of any of us getting off easy in that way—we will all, in fact, reap what we sow. But God is not the cosmic enforcer of karma, making sure we get what we deserve. God is the one who interrupts this cycle with grace.

Sin does not keep God away from us—we cannot outrun his everlasting love. But what our own choices can do is blind us so our vision of God is a distortion. The God we see through the lens of duty and obligation, through the lens of bad religion, is not the God we are actually offered in Jesus of Nazareth. So many of the teachings of Jesus gesture toward this—that God is not who we have always presumed him to be. In the famous story of the prodigal son, the wayward boy squanders his father's inheritance and thus has to live with the consequences of his actions; therefore he finds himself working in a hog pen. Significantly, it is only when he "came to himself" that he began to remember his father for who he really is and has always been.[13]

But even then, it is "through a glass, darkly."[14] This lost son thinks the only way his father will allow him to come home is as a hired hand. He does not know yet that his father only wants to tackle him with ferocious love, embrace him, and celebrate his return. But as much as the father wants his son home, the one thing he will not do is force him to stay there. Even though he knows his son will have to learn some hard lessons through his choices, they are yet very much his own choices to make. So the father does give his son the inheritance—even though he knows it will be squandered.

The cross of Jesus says to us there is nothing God won't do to bring us home—except force us to choose him. The cross is God laying down his great power so we might be compelled by the beauty of his heart. He will not coerce us, but only woo us. And yet as long as we see Jesus through the distorted lens of bad religion, every invitation is perceived as a threat.

> The cross is God laying down his great power so we might be compelled by the beauty of his heart.

That night sitting in the restaurant after I read that section in *Broken Open*, I had a revelation I don't think I'll ever get over: Up to that point in my life, I had never really chosen God. I was still the little boy who thought the cable repairman's blood was going to be on my hands if I didn't share my testimony. I was still living a life motivated by fear rather than love. It was not God who was coercing me, but my own terror of God—which, ironically enough, kept me from being able to truly love him. Because when we feel like we do not have a choice, choosing God is not yet possible. I heard the whisper of the Holy Spirit, a scandal to my own ears: "You don't have to choose me—but I would sure love for you to do so."

By that point in my life, I had preached countless sermons about the love, grace, and beauty of God that is revealed in Jesus. And yet in my own deepest self, I still saw him as a punitive ogre. I still had not learned that my own bad choices did not change God's heart for me, but rather my perception of God. Hell would be to remain forever caught in such a delusion, unable to see God for who and how he really is.

God is the God of the sea, the one who plays in the depths. It is only in our own depths that we could come to know such a God. "When I was a child, I spoke like a child, I thought like a child, I reasoned like a child; when I became an adult, I put an end to childish ways," Paul wrote.[15] As long as we are caught in childish, infantile delusions about God, we remain trapped in the most primitive level of consciousness—that of fear and law. "Don't do that because I told you not to." That is a life lived in the shallows, if it can be called a life at all.

You Can't Outrun God

Christian theology says that God is the one who actively sustains all life—everything that exists, right here, right now: "In him we live and move and have our being."[16] Everything that is alive is alive because of God, and he is the one who holds all things together. He is in everything—in the sky and the dirt and the wind and the waves and the trees and the grass and the flowers all around us. That is not to say God is those things (that's pantheism—"God is the tree, so we should worship the tree"). But he certainly is *in* all those things, and everything else, giving life and breath and being, holding the creation together in all of its unity and diversity.

There is no getting around that God. There is no getting away from that God. If you exist (and the fact that you are reading this means you do!), the reality of God is all around you, no matter what you call it or don't call it. So the idea that you have to make all the right choices to get to God cannot be true. God is the reason you have a brain competent enough to make decisions at all. God is the reason you have legs you can use to walk through any doors at all. God is the reason there are doors—the reason there are choices—and people to walk through them. God is in all of it, all the time. God is the reason you are able to "be" at all, and nothing you say or do changes that fact. Or changes the fact that he sees you and knows you for who and what you really are, and that he loves you with an infinite love, as David reminds us in Psalms. These things are not just true; they are foundational truths of human existence, and they are true for all people in all places.

So let's be clear: There is no door you will ever walk through that, somewhere, somehow, will leave you unable to seek God, call out for him, find him. That is not a way of saying "all paths lead to God" or "all paths lead to heaven" or that there aren't real differences between the different paths you might choose. That is not to say there are no consequences to your actions. That is not to say there aren't better or worse doors to walk through or some decisions that are better and healthier to make. That is not to say there are not some doors that will lead to helping you become more aware of that divine presence that constantly envelops you while eating, drinking, sleeping, working, and being, and some doors that will lead you away from being awake to that presence. Our choices matter a great deal, probably more than we've ever dared to believe.

> There is no door you will ever walk through that, somewhere, somehow, will leave you unable to seek God, call out for him, find him.

Yet this should take at least some of the pressure off, especially for those of us who feel like somehow we have gone off script from the life we felt we were supposed to have. No matter where you are currently or where you're heading, you aren't going to outrun God. You aren't going to escape God. God is faster and stronger than you are. You can't so offend him or annoy him to make him run off from you forever. And for whatever other things are at stake with the choices you make, I can assure you that the unconditional love that God has for you as his child is not up for negotiation at any time or in any place.

We still have a lot of choices to make, a lot to figure out about what kind of people we're going to become and what sorts of things we're going to do. You still have to make decisions about what to do with that fractured relationship, whether or not to stay in that dead-end job, what to do about those complicated children—oh, and still figure out where to go for lunch and whether to have a sandwich or a salad. I get that. I just think it's important to establish that God is not on the other side of any particular door passively waiting; he is on the other side of all the doors, eager to be discovered, and better yet, he is on this side of the door with you right here, right now—for you and not against you.

Part of the good news is that since there is no way to escape God or outrun God—no matter where you are in life—there are no dead ends. I'm very much the product of African-American preaching, and as the old black preachers always said, "God will make a way where there is no way!" Even when we go through a door that leads to nowhere, God is possibility. God is always making available new opportunities to us. In the words of Parker Palmer, "Each time a door closes, the rest of the world opens up."[17]

So how about all these choices?

If God is everywhere—if God is being itself—then the world is open to us in so many ways. But we are not just people who are going around trying to unlock doors. We started from the premise that we all, on some level, want to unlock God himself. God is the mystery we are really chasing after, whether or not we understand that, and no matter where we are looking. I love this quote, often attributed to G. K. Chesterton but actually found in a book by Scottish novelist Bruce Marshall: "The young man who rings the bell at the brothel is unconsciously looking for God."[18] Whether you think you are looking for *more sex with great-looking people* or *more money* or *the big promotion*, God is what you're really looking for, whether or not you know how to name that desire.

So then, part of what it means to unlock God surely is to figure out what this divine being (who is being itself) wants us to do and then do it, right? We have to figure out what God's plan for us really is. If you've been in church for any amount of time in your life, you've probably heard this phrase before: "God loves you and has a wonderful plan for your life." Here's the thing: I think God is hopelessly in love with you. And I do think God wants your life to be wonderful, insofar as he wants your life to have a sense of deep meaning and fulfillment, even happiness in the ancient sense of the word. But I also think there is a tremendous amount of pressure that either we put on ourselves or others put on us to walk through that right door, as if finding God has to do with making sure we find the right spouse, the right job, the right car, the right outfit for Tuesday's meeting. And of course, it follows that if we do not marry the "right" person, get the "right" job, walk through door number three instead of doors number one and two—well, I'm sorry. You are out on your own, out of the script, out of the will. Good luck finding your way back to "the path."

I don't think anything could be further from the truth. As a matter of fact—even though this is going to be a challenge for some of you—I would say it like this: God does not have a highly detailed, overly scripted individual plan for your life. A life lived in constant anxiety about whether or not you've found the perfect path or the one and only unique script is no life at all—because such a thing does not exist. It never has. It is the well-intentioned (if not entirely innocent) product of a culture obsessed with individuality.

Note what I did not say. I did not say God does not have good plans for you. I did not say God does not have a will for your life. I did not say God is indifferent to the choices you make or the kind of person you become. I said he doesn't have an individual plan for all of us. There is a kind of comfort in thinking you've been handed a tight script, but there's a terrible monotony to it too. You're not a pawn on a chessboard, mindlessly being moved by a higher power. You are called to be "God's fellow workers."[19] You get a say in the kind of life you want to live, the kind of person you want to become, the kind of work you want to do.

It's an intimidating prospect, I know. We often don't know what we really want—or even if we do, we often want things that are not best for us. That is a real problem. But what if there was a life we could live where we were in touch with our deepest desires, the ones implanted in us before we were born? Not the desire to be popular or wealthy or have sex with whomever we want—but the things our souls most deeply long for, the things our hearts most deeply crave?

> What if there was a life we could live where we were in touch with our deepest desires, the ones implanted in us before we were born?

No matter what you are doing or what kind of life you are choosing, that's the kind of life you are looking for, whether or not you know you are looking for it. It's *the* desire that runs underneath the desire—the quiet but powerful rushing stream that runs beneath all your conscious choices and deepest dreams. It's why the Bruce Marshall quote about the brothel rings so true within us.

And the more you allow that deeper desire to bubble to the surface, shaping you, shifting you, moving you, the freer you become. That's what makes possible the kind of life Saint Augustine described: "Love God, and do what you will."[20]

There was a popular country song a few years ago called "Jesus, Take the Wheel." I get what the song is trying to communicate—it's about letting go of your life and letting God steer your life for you. There is a kind of truth to that—a life with God does start with letting Jesus "take the wheel." But that is just one part of the story of the Christian life; it is certainly not the whole story. The truth of the story is a lot more exciting—and a lot more terrifying—than that: Jesus wants to teach us how to drive.

Heaven help us. That might feel like a lot of pressure. But before you go running out of the classroom, take a deep breath. God does want to teach you, to lead you, to direct you. God does not want you to attempt to drive on your own or make decisions on your own. That is why he sent us the Holy Spirit—the actual living presence of Jesus—to not only sit beside us in the car but to dwell within us. And that is why we are given the gift of wise friends who have the Holy Spirit within them too. They, like us, can be horrible backseat drivers. But they can also keep us from accidents and speeding tickets.

I don't want to leave the driving analogy behind, because I think it's accessible to most of us. Years ago, a bumper sticker popped up everywhere that read, "God is my copilot." That became the fodder for a thousand sermons. For a while, almost every pastor in America seemed to find a way to work in the line, "If God is your copilot, honey, you are in the wrong seat!" It was a good line. Catchy. It worked as a quip. And if the idea of having God as your copilot means you are attempting to take the place of Jesus as Lord and be your own ultimate source of authority—yeah, displacing God is always a bad idea. He knows an awful lot more than we do. But if the reality is that life itself is God's own invitation to teach us how to fly, to learn how to read the instrument panel, to recognize the weather patterns, to learn to cooperate with the wind—then we aren't displacing God at all, but we're doing precisely what he has created and even called us to do.

In case you're afraid of flying, let's bring the metaphor back down to earth for a moment. When I was a kid, my grandfather used to take me out on the riding lawn mower and let me "drive." I got to put my little hands on the steering wheel. I got to turn the lawn mower to the right or to the left (though I could not turn it very hard). But I was sitting in his lap, and he was doing the heavy lifting. He was in charge, and I was safe to steer precisely because he was there. Yet in a very real way, I was in the driver's seat. Even though I was much weaker and much smaller, I was invited to drive the lawn mower with him. Not because I was arrogant and was trying to usurp his authority, but because it was in his good nature to want me to have a part, to want to share something of his adult "power" with me.

Cars, airplanes, lawn mowers—you get the idea: Part of how God wants to share his life with us is through sharing his power to choose, to steer, to drive.

Chapter Seven

Don't Fight the Wind

Be still:
There is no longer any need of comment.
It was a lucky wind
That blew away his halo with his cares,
A lucky sea that drowned his reputation.

Thomas Merton

The ultimate terror that comes in the shipwreck does not come from the depths in the form of any monster—or even in the waves that threaten to overtake you—but in the loss of control. To watch the boards give way beneath your feet, the moment . . . just before you know you're going overboard? Nothing could ever be more terrifying than that. You are not, at this point, exactly making a decision to let go—you are feeling the world that you've known and loved ripped from your hands. The wind and the sea are not gentle, but violent. And what happens at first is not just an unclenching of your hands; it is a tearing, a ripping. And you feel the tear right in the center of you, the veil that protected your true self from the elements outside torn from top to bottom.

And yet, for whatever malevolent forces seem to be conspiring against you, there is a benevolent force in the wind too—something in the storm that has not come to tear you. When the Spirit is first poured out on the church in Acts 2, she does not come gentle—she does not manifest as a dove. Instead, "a sound like the rush of a violent wind" fills the house.[1] The sound of the hurricane was the sound of the Spirit filling the room. Beneath the noise—the splitting of the wood and of your own heart—listen closer. Is the Spirit blowing in on the wind to you, even while the ship is still going down? To be clear, I don't believe God causes the storm, or the shipwreck. And yet I do not know how to extricate the chaos of the sea from the chaos in God. I do not know why it is that the same violent wind that blows your house down is also the wind that carries in the Spirit to you.

When the Spirit blows in, the first sign of the divine presence is not order, but confusion. When the early disciples were filled with the Spirit and began to speak in other tongues, the world around them was bewildered. It is the first and most neglected sign that God is up to something extraordinary—bewilderment. I have come to feel much better about people who are bewildered than I do about people who approach their lives with too much certainty. If you feel too sure, you are probably living with a false sense of control. Only the people who don't know what they are doing or where their lives are headed are open to the Spirit in the wind. The trademark of the Spirit is to first bewilder, not clarify. The fog that comes doesn't always obscure the Spirit—sometimes it *is* the Spirit. To welcome Pentecost is to open ourselves to the possibility that God may be working in that which at first only appears to be confusion.

It is not that the Spirit is the cause of the chaos, but that she is at home in it, which is a way of also saying she is at home in you. The chaos does not originate from the Spirit, but she does brood over it—she hovers over it. This is where the story of God begins: "In the beginning when God created the heavens and the earth, the earth was a formless void and darkness covered the face of the deep, *while a wind from God swept over the face of the waters.*"[2] In the storm, somehow, the Spirit of God sweeps over the face of us, sweeps over our depths—coming to bring some kind of order out of the chaos, some kind of form into the formlessness of our sea. Sometimes she comes as a breeze blowing softly against your face—but sometimes in the violence of the wind. The "chaosmos," in James Joyce's phrase,[3] where there is nothing but disorder and upheaval, is the place of new life, the place of creation. We have to stay there long enough to let the wind of God brood over our depths.

> The trademark of the Spirit is to first bewilder, not clarify. The fog that comes doesn't always obscure the Spirit— sometimes it *is* the Spirit.

When the violent wind blows over us, we can decide if we are willing to bend, to adapt—or let the wind break us utterly. We can live as if we should be in a position to determine the weather or accept that it is out of our control, that we are just here to surf. Many people stiffen when the storm comes and refuse to move with the wind and with the waves. This may seem noble at first—like some kind of courageous resolve. But often this amounts to a kind of sanctified denial that will not change the storm but will devastate us.

I'm all for wishful thinking. I just don't think it's worth making a religion out of. In my tradition, I've seen people set their faces against the wind and when the bad report comes, they say, "I don't receive that." When the son or daughter comes home and announces an unplanned pregnancy or they're gay or they're not going down the career path Mom or Dad had hoped for, they say, "I don't receive that." But being unbendable is not the marker of walking in faith; being adaptable is. We only harm ourselves when we insist that the world around us is not working as it should be. God is at work not in the world as it should be but in the world that actually is. God is never in the ideas, abstractions, concepts, notions, or ideals. God is at work in reality; God is at work in the real.

With the roar of the ocean in our ears, the dissonance between the world as we thought we knew it and the world as it is now destroys our equilibrium. We want to ball up our fists toward the sky and scream that this is not the way it is supposed to be—and there is nothing wrong with doing that if you need to. But when you come to yourself, again . . . listen to the whisper of the Spirit: "Are we going to talk about the world as you think it should be or the world as it actually is?" Is having faith—or expressing trust—to insist on a particular outcome? Or is it instead to ask ourselves the question—since *this is*, and God is only at work in what actually is—"What is the invitation here . . . now?"

On the other side of the shipwreck, there is no room for rigidity. We will become people of the Spirit, people of the wind, endlessly flexible and adaptable—or we will not survive out here. We must learn, not to rely on the facts, but to hone our instincts, to find the Spirit in the wind and in the waves. No matter how much we might like or not like the world as we know it now, surely God is at work in it somehow. Surely then, there is an invitation to life and to grace, even in this—even now.

"If the Dog Drowns, You Don't Want Him"

The first business the wind has when she blows over you is to eliminate the clutter of all you think you need but don't need that much after all—to remove everything based on illusion or deception. This feels violent, because it is. It is the deconstruction before there can be construction, the bewilderment that must come before the clarity, the tearing down that must occur before the building up. The wind strains, hard, against all that you thought you knew, pulling up every pillar and hurling every brick that wasn't built to survive the storm. To a point, you have to allow this to happen. In some ways, the most terrible part of the experience of shipwreck is allowing yourself to be powerless to fix things you think ought to be fixed. You have to let everything shake that can be shaken, in the imagery used by the author of Hebrews.[4] If the relationship can be shaken, it needs to shake. If the job can be shaken, it needs to shake. If the religious belief system can be shaken, it *definitely* needs to shake!

My friend Tim Gilbert and his wife, Barbara, from New Orleans, are like a second set of parents to me among the small group of people who helped me survive my own shipwreck. Tim is retired now, a man who has lived as fascinating and full a life as anybody I know (fun trivia: Tim wrote the 1967 rock hit "Incense and Peppermints" sung by Strawberry Alarm Clock). His stories have meant a lot to me through the long, dark season for different reasons. One of my favorite stories is about his growing-up years in Denver, when he and his brother spent their summers working on boats. One summer, they needed to get a dog that would be able to retrieve boat bumpers from the water. So that spring as a teenager, he and his younger brother went up to a river in the mountains, to a crusty old man who trained dogs for that task. The dog the man had been training was just a puppy, and Tim and his brother immediately fell in love with him. They set out together in the boat to witness the dog's big test. The runoff in the spring is especially violent, so when the man ordered the dog to jump into the water, Tim's little brother started to cry. As they watched the puppy's black head bobbing up and down as he struggled to swim downstream, he got even more upset. So he looked up at the old curmudgeon and asked, through tears, "But what if the dog drowns?" The man looked him dead in the eye and said, "Son, if the dog drowns, you don't want him."

I'm a dog lover, so of course the story made me cringe. But it hit me hard at the time because of its hard, stark truth. In Tim's story, thankfully the puppy made it. But all dogs do not survive. And the point, of course, is that if the dog wasn't equipped for the task, this would be the only way to find out. I put myself in Tim's brother's shoes, watching through tears from the back of the boat, hoping to God that the puppy's black head would keep coming up out of the water, that the current would not take him under—knowing there was nothing in the world I could do for him, letting the emotionless river have its way. Is there anything more terrible?

The fact is, shipwreck is not a time when sentimentality or illusions can hold you up; it's a time for truth, a time to look at things you'd rather avoid. Sometimes that means you can't just listen to the voice of "reason"; the time of shipwreck forces you to learn to listen to your gut. You have to look at things, most of all yourself, for what they are and what you are, not for what they should be and what you should be. Hollow consolations and fabricated encouragement will not help. In the shipwreck, *what is*, is always your friend.

Snake Charmer

I am, by nature, a relentless optimist, which you might not gather from reading this book! But it is my default setting. It has its perks but also a lot of downside when it comes to looking at hard realities I'd rather not have to come to terms with. That has been the root of so many issues in my life—my inability to look at the dark side, to stare into the black eyes of the monsters in myself or others.

The uncompromising wind of the storm will correct this, whether or not you ask for it. The wind carries you where you need to go, to see what you need to see—if you let it. If you attempt to repress this inward journey by day, your dreams will take you into these places by night. But one way or another, your eyes will be opened, even if pried. For all the harsh realities of the shipwreck, the gift is almost always the gift of *seeing*—of being opened to new ways to see the world and to see yourself in ways you did not have the courage to see before.

Often, the things we have been running from and denied have to be accepted. Part of what it means to make peace with God and with ourselves is to make peace with the world around us in all of its wildness. Instead of compartmentalizing unpleasant truths about ourselves and the lives we've been given, we accept the limitations of our own creatureliness—and have the opportunity now to integrate them into our lives and into our stories. It is only the grace of God that makes this possible, allowing us to see both ourselves and people around us with compassion rather than judgment. This is the opportunity for us to finally stop beating against the waves and cursing them, and stop fighting against the tide, incessantly. This is the acceptance that can bring us to shores of peace, allowing us to receive life in its profound brokenness as a gift. We are learning to accept the world as it is instead of as we think it should be—and to still love unflinchingly. In this way, the shipwreck is a sacred invitation to come and experience the world as God does, with heartbreak and tears, to be sure—and yet with perfect love that casts out all fear.

Because the things we have been afraid to see truthfully rule over us, the wind carries us straight into the dark center of the unknowing to confront the wildness of created things. It was on the far side of my shipwreck, as I was just starting to feel the wind shift, that I started driving up to Crowder's Mountain, near my old house, to hike and pray every day. It was strange the way the mountain itself seemed to summon me, as if I could hear the whisper of the Spirit—as to Moses on Mount Sinai—"If you come here, I will meet you."[5] So day after day, I climbed the mountain, not expecting tablets engraved from heaven, but hoping to have some kind of encounter with God. And as it always is when God actually manifests in some way, I was ultimately surprised at how he did.

It was near my last days in North Carolina, the only home I had known for thirty-seven years. One morning when I got up, I specifically felt the Spirit was impressing on me that God wanted to deal with me about fear—about the things I was really, deeply, truly afraid of. So I had this in mind when I started up the trail. Five minutes into the hike, I saw the biggest snake I'd ever seen in real life— outside of at the zoo!—right in front of me. I froze. I have a dread fear of snakes, and at any other time in my life, I would have run for the other side of the trail. But I was fascinated, intrigued, almost touched by the snake. I realized he belonged on this mountain, in this ecosystem, every bit as much as I did. He had a place there. So instead of running, I leaned in closer, watching him, observing him, learning from him. I took a few pictures with my phone. The invitation of the Spirit seemed clear: Don't be afraid to look at the snake. This is the time in your life when you have to learn to be okay with beholding the snake, seeing him for what he is, knowing he has a place.

The former version of me would have avoided the snake, dodged the snake, perhaps pretended the snake did not exist. But now, for the first time in my life, there was a place to accept the snake and to accept that beholding the creatures within and without that I had not been comfortable with was what this season was all about. No running, no hiding, no pretending—to look at the snake unguarded, without fear. This was the Spirit's invitation in that moment. This is how the Spirit always comes to us—through the invitation to see reality before us, as it really is, yet with love and with grace. I saw that the snake belonged here, same as I did. I saw that the snake had a function and a role in this ecosystem. I did not judge it, nor did I run away in fear. I was not reacting any longer with the wild, desperate panic I would have reacted with before the shipwreck. I could now study the snake and learn from it. God was no longer confined to sacred space but could be seen in the whole of the mountain and in its inhabitants.

I do not propose that anyone looks into the eyes of the abyss just for the sake of the staring. But what made it safe to look at everything I could not look at before was that now, like never before, my soul was finally making a home in God. I'm not exactly sure where or how that happened, except to say my own desperation forced me into God in ways I could not have imagined before. I was discovering the love at the very bottom of things. What is there left to be afraid of when we know that God lives down here, that

Love lives down here? In the safety of God's presence over me like a canopy, there is room now for snakes and sea monsters—for the wildness of creation. These beasts, like me, originate in God, and to God surely we all go back. Steadily growing more comfortable in the fundamental rhythm of creation, then, I could breathe, open my eyes, and look. It is fear that makes us choose blindness, that makes us want to bury our heads in the sand. Grace is the only thing that gives us courage enough and strength

> Grace is the only thing that gives us courage enough and strength enough to live with eyes wide open.

enough to live with eyes wide open. Grace gives us hearts big enough to accept creation—and ourselves—in brokenness and fragility instead of despising it.

Resuscitation or Resurrection

During my shipwreck, I found myself returning over and over to an encounter I had just weeks before I left our church. I was in a hospital room for Heather, one of the people I would baptize a few weeks later on my last Sunday at Renovatus. Her father looked impossibly alive. To see the strength in the six-foot-four frame of this sixtyish African-American man, to see the color in his cheeks and feel the warmth in his large hands, it was hard to believe he could be dying.

Two months prior, he had fallen at work and suffered serious head trauma. The doctors didn't know if he would survive, but after several serious and complex surgeries, he was finally on the mend. In fact, he was no longer in a regular hospital room but in a rehabilitation ward—days from going home—until out of nowhere, he had a heart attack in his bed. They were able to resuscitate him, but he had been without oxygen for too long—he was completely brain-dead. The part of Herman where all the memories and motor functions resided was not going to come back. He was only breathing because of a ventilator, and this precious family was trying to make the terrible, necessary decision to pull the plug on the artificial life support that was sustaining him.

I held his enormous hand as the family pressed in behind me. The holiness of the ground itself was almost unbearable. The spiritual transition taking place was palpable, and everyone in the room could feel it. Herman's life was fading away, and it was time for the people he loved to send him off. I closed my eyes to lead the family in prayer, feeling the hot tears roll quietly down my face as we sensed the beauty and sorrow of the moment pressing in on us. The more I prayed, the more the family began to lean into the prayer—with tears, with soft amens, with resolved yes, Lords.

Hours later in my home, I felt the familiar presence again, and I knew there was something I was supposed to see while still saturated in the holiness of Herman's departure. Once again, the presence was tender. Once again, the words, while gentle, were also hard. I was once again seeing what I did not want to see. In the twinkling of an eye, I saw that in my life back at the church, I was choosing resuscitation. I saw that my chest was still heaving with air; I was still warm to the touch; and I could still hold someone else's hand in my own—but there was no life for me there anymore. I was a ghost, refusing to depart from my old life. I was a dead man insisting he was not dead.

It struck me that night what a terribly courageous thing the family had to do. They did not know any better than the rest of us that Herman would be resurrected if they let him go—they had not been on the other side of that transition any more than the rest of us have. But they chose to believe it. They chose to put their weight down on the hope of resurrection. They chose to say good-bye to a semblance of life, the form of life, in the hope of Herman experiencing the substance of life on the other side. They did not choose resuscitation; they chose resurrection. I knew I did not possess their bravery, and that I doubted myself as much as they believed for Herman. I did know I trusted the God of resurrection and had no problems placing weight down on that hope with them for Herman. But I did not know if I could trust it for myself. I only knew I was being faced with the same choice.

Two days later, I had one more moment when I felt strangely inclined to pull a book off the shelf. This time, it was my own. I will always love that first book, because it came from some deep places. It was honest to where I was—it was true to the first half of my life. I stand by everything in it. But those were things I knew so much more with my head than with my heart, uplifting information that was still turning into revelation inside of me.

I gave each chapter one-word titles, and there was a somewhat linear movement and progression to them, a kind of flow. From identity . . . to beloved . . . to wilderness . . . to calling . . . to wounds . . . to resurrection . . . to . . .—I stopped myself. I was looking at the pages and was overcome with that terrible knowing, the kind that comes when the Spirit enters the room. The kind that comes from being shown what you do not want to see. The kind that "flesh and blood has not revealed . . . to you, but my Father in heaven."[6] My eyes filled again with tears, but it was so perfectly obvious that I couldn't help but smile at my own ignorance, however disastrous it might feel now. I had written a book on Christian spirituality, of which death and resurrection are its central motifs and defining characteristics—and had moved straight from wounds to resurrection. There was nothing in that book about death, because I did not yet know what it would mean to die.

That was the chapter of my life finally being written.

Writing Your Own Death Chapter

Some fires that dwindle in our lives are meant to be rekindled. Other times, it is necessary to let some of the old fires die out and be led into a new place where there are to be new flames. Only the Spirit can give us the discernment to know the difference. Perhaps some fires are waning in your life—fires simply in need of more kindling and some fresh fire. If that is the case, by all means, rekindle the flame; don't let it die out.

But in my experience of shipwrecks—others' as much as my own—some deaths are necessary, even though so painful. And it is not a matter of giving up hope or giving up the fight; it is a way of acknowledging the truth and of putting hard-edged hope down—on the hope of resurrection. It is not about fairy tales, optimism, or pipe dreams; it is about acting in full confidence that we have a God who still raises from the dead and thus leaves us a world where there are no dead ends. Even the end is hardly the end for the love that overwhelms death.

> What looks like resignation may be the ultimate act of faith, the supreme expression of trust.

And yet even so, coming to the end of anything—the end of an era, the end of a relationship, the end of ourselves—is so horribly frightening when you are on the front side of resurrection. I am not encouraging you to go kill anything that is still alive—and dare God to resurrect it. But I would encourage you, softly and gently, to consider carefully anything in your life that is half-dead—existing on a ventilator. And to at least be open to the possibility that it could be time to unplug the ventilator. Not as an act of cowardice or an act of resignation, but as an act of bold, courageous faith—putting all your weight down on the hope of resurrection.

What looks like resignation may be the ultimate act of faith, the supreme expression of trust. And what you are keeping on life support may be exactly the thing that is keeping you from the wonder and terror of new life.

Chapter Eight

Starting to See

Compassion is the sometimes fatal capacity for feeling what it's like to live inside somebody else's skin. It's the knowledge that there can never really be any peace and joy for me until there is peace and joy finally for you too.

Frederick Buechner

I have a theory that has been rustling around in my brain these last few years that I kind of hate to speak aloud, because I assume people are going to hate it as much as I would have before the shipwreck. I hardly think I'm Columbus discovering America with any of this to begin with—I always feel these days like I'm stumbling onto truths that have been perfectly obvious to every human being who has lived awake in any time and place, ever. Then again, Columbus didn't actually know it was America he was discovering, so maybe there is something to be said for playing the part of the clueless discoverer of new parts of your own soul and of worlds you didn't know existed. Just because a couple million people got here before me doesn't mean I don't get to delight in the wonder of seeing what I could not have seen before. The theory I sailed to, better late than never, is essentially this: God can only be truthfully experienced from the underside of things.

It seems perfectly plain to me now. But it was hiding in plain sight, the way the truth always is before loss, failure, and suffering open our eyes to it. The God story is always the minority report of the people who have felt themselves trampled—by the chariots of the pharaoh, by the consequences of their own actions, by the Babylonian Empire, by white colonial invaders, by Jim Crow laws. Everyone who has ever had soul found it when their lives were being squeezed out—from the hymns of the ancient Israelites to the African-American spirituals of the 1800s. I've always enjoyed soul music in the way tourists and outsiders do, in the way cultured citizens of the empire do—as a novelty, as a cultural artifact, but never from the inside. It's much easier to appreciate soul music than to make it, but soul music requires us to embrace our pain, own it, incorporate it.

> It's much easier to appreciate soul music than to make it, but soul music requires us to embrace our pain, own it, incorporate it.

I grew up in a fiery Pentecostal world where black preaching stirred whatever was inside me like nothing else could. Later, I fell in love with hip-hop. The first CD I owned was by A Tribe Called Quest. I went through long stages of trying to dress like my favorite urban artists through middle and early high school, with the awkwardness only someone this pale and already a gangly six foot four at fourteen years old could have managed. As I became older, a long, sustained study of Martin Luther King Jr. and the

Civil Rights Movement captured my imagination, even if I did not have the courage or the instincts to live into the revolution of the ideas the way I wanted to. I loved to go and visit my friend John P. Kee's church in Charlotte and let the Hammond B-3 organ shake my insides. I loved all kinds of gospel music—but as a spectator who never quite found my own shout. Because shouting is as unintelligible as suffering, when you have the luxury of living the whole of life without a shipwreck. I could imitate black preaching in the shower, the way some people can sing a little opera in the shower, but was in no danger of living the highs and lows of black preaching—or the highs and lows of the opera either.

I needed to find the voice I had, the one that had soul in it. But all the while, I was still living the superficial life one lives on the topside of everything, the privileged life of someone who always has a seat at the table for the big conversations without having to ask for it. This didn't seem so bad, because I always lived in the world with such a wonderfully vague, generalized care for all humans every-where, theoretically including those who suffered. I always cared—in the polite, detached, latently condescending way people do for people they don't understand—about the poor, about people with AIDS, about homosexuals, about anybody pushed to the margins of any circle anywhere. And I would loan my educated, white voice to them whenever I could—as long as it didn't cost me too much personally.

The only trouble with this is that loving people from afar is little more than a way of purging your conscience, a way of alleviating your guilt. It's the soulless solidarity of the vaguely interested, all that anybody can manage before they learn how to be in touch with their own pain. The only God who could save us was the God who suffered, the "man of sorrows, and acquainted with grief."[1] I avoided casual interactions with grief, even at cocktail parties; I did not know any particular sorrows on a first-name basis. Virtually nobody who lives like this is capable of being self-aware about it, which is why it is absolutely fine if you are reading this to think this is all ridiculous. Who wouldn't—until the bough breaks and the cradle falls, and down come your dreams, cradle and all?

It doesn't matter how well-intentioned you are—I have always had good intentions for days. There are things that cannot be seen about God and life and the world and yourself from on top. Until you can see it all from flat on your back, you just aren't seeing much at all. The tale told from the ones who inherited the land by birthright rather than by the spilling of their own blood is never entirely truthful, no matter how honestly we try to tell it. That world produces music critics, but not original music; that world produces words, but doesn't create sound. When not only have you not experienced shipwreck but have barely even yet been out to sea, you can't truly see anyone else. You haven't even really seen yourself yet.

Seeing through the Lens of Our Own Brokenness

The only way our vision can be whole is to see the world through the lens of our brokenness. As long as we pretend we are not broken, we can't trust our own vision. We see the world in a funhouse mirror that shrinks our own faults and exaggerates flaws in others. We see through the lenses of pride, ego, and competition. We cannot merely make a decision to see the world differently; something has to happen to make us go blind first.

This is why it's useless to try to make ourselves or anyone else see the world with more empathy and compassion. That kind of seeing is not native to us in our self-interest; it is the gift only trauma can give us. People don't just wake up one day and decide to see the world through the lens of grace—and suddenly want to change the world. We aren't able to engage the world differently until we are disillusioned with the way we saw ourselves before, until we begin to doubt the integrity of our old way of seeing.

Nobody sees the world differently until life happens to them and the illusory lines of set-apartness are blurred by our pain. It is true we have much more in common with the person we most see as "other" in how we experience joy and pleasure, but very rarely does shared joy illuminate how similar we are to the people we feel most set apart from. It is only when we see we bleed the same way, taste the same saltwater tears, break in all the same places, that the lines between us and them are finally erased. It would be wonderful if we could become enlightened enough, educated enough, sophisticated enough, to see the world from high above—and have some kind of aerial perspective on it. But the only entirely truthful way we will ever see the world will not be while floating above it, but seeing the world from flat on our backs.

The Terrible Gift of Sight

I had spent the exact amount of time looking at God and life from the bottom that I had spent under the bottom of the car (that would be zero minutes). But as a church boy who had more or less done well at everything I tried to do—in my denomination, in seminary, in planting a church—I always got to sit at the table where the people with influence get to decide who does and does not belong at the Lord's Table. I always knew the table of Jesus is the table spread for the outsiders. I always knew that the table is spread for all. I always fought, in the small ways I could, for anyone who had felt excluded to find a place there. And yet I see now how, with again my buckets of good intentions, how much my lack of real-life, real-world experience made me inadequate to the task, how social position alone was enough to guarantee I could only be so reliable in such matters.

I could not sleep. In a few hours, it would be time to preach twice in my own pulpit. Tired of lying awake alone in the guest bedroom, I finally turned on the lamp beside my bed. It had been five months since the world I had built had gone up in flames, and it was all my fault. It was like a Hollywood makeup artist had transformed me during those long months—I saw the shadows underneath my eyes getting larger, watched the white hairs in my beard turn into wildfire, and picked a big clump of my once thick, dark brown hair out of the drain in the shower every morning. I didn't know how I was going to get up and face them again, much less my own face in the mirror.

I picked up the John Irving novel from the bedside table, the one with the black-and-white cover showing a woman's back as she unlatched her bra. Only when I read the novel, *In One Person*, I found out it was actually a man. I picked up the paperback in an airport a few months ago, knowing nothing about the story and only knowing I loved the author.

Before the storm, I read about half of it. And to my shame, I put it down.

The story of a young boy growing up in an all-boys school in New England and trying to sort out his sexual identity moved me. But it was the first book I'd ever read where the protagonist was gay or bisexual. It was foreign to me, and quite honestly, I simply didn't know what to do with such bodily frankness.

So now I picked it back up that night, in a very different place in my life. I wasn't upwardly mobile anymore. I was out to sea. I was trying to sort out all these issues of life and my marriage while still in the pastorate, feeling myself dying slowly and not wanting to be there but feeling responsible to the people and to this thing we had built. I didn't know how to leave, but I didn't know how to be present either. I was still trying to find a way to be vulnerable in the sermons without being indiscreet about the particulars of my situation. I felt like I was slowly bleeding out in front of everybody.

I picked up a book about conflicting passions, and it illumined all of my own. Irving's novel was grounded in very real historical events—the AIDS epidemic among gay men in New York City in the 1980s. As the lead character loses friend after friend to the plague, the heartbreak of the book overwhelmed me. I grieved over the deaths I read about. I grieved over the pain of rejection he and his friends endured. Three hours later, I had finished the novel and was just sitting cross-legged in the middle of the bed, sobbing. I cried for many reasons. I cried because after taking four months to try to sort out our lives, I was nowhere close to resolution. I cried because the angst in the novel both massaged and stirred up all the angst in me.

Being raised Pentecostal, I have always believed God was speaking, not to me in particular, but to all of us, and that there were moments when my antenna was up when I could hear something. Ironically, the reception seemed to be clearer in a storm, even in one of my own making. It is difficult to quantify how it is I think I hear from God, but it is as though words settle within me that—for lack of a better way of putting it—just feel altogether other. It is a deep, interior way of knowing, perceiving, listening, that I fade in and out of. When the familiar voice comes, it is marked by tenderness—there is something sweet about it, and yet almost something that breaks my heart too, in all the ways pure love does.

That night, I saw something I did not want to see. I saw I was loving people from a distance—because their situations were complicated and boldly messy and just too precarious—when God had paid the ultimate price to come near. Before then, would I have allowed myself to be as broken for anyone in my real life as I was with a character in a novel? It had started out earnestly, but I had become too busy with safe Christian work, vaguely caring but too clinically detached, having an impervious bedside manner. I was too cautious in navigating the complicated politics of ecclesial life, still very much a voice for love and compassion generally but avoiding any particulars that could get me into trouble. That meant a kind of loving people from a distance.

I was broken open simply because I now had my own pain, my own unresolved inner conflict, neck-deep in my own angst. And I was finally learning to see the world again, to truly see people. People who, like me, are complicated and messy and tangled in a terrible way. I finally was starting to see God again in the only way people ever can—from the underside of things. I was no longer in a place of power, deciding what was up or down or in or out, no longer at the head of the table, participating in a lively discussion about who else should or should not be there. I was now hoping I was still in a place to get a few scraps from it—but I was not sure.

I wept when I finished the novel because I knew I had held a lot of people and a lot of pain at arm's length before my own slow-motion fall. And I heard the words of Jesus spoken to Peter, gently naming the reality of my own heart—I had been the one who knew what it was to be in charge, to take care of myself, to take care of others. But now was the time when others would have to "dress you and lead you where you do not want to go."[2] I now had the terrible gift of sight. I could not avoid real-life stories anymore just because I was afraid of where they might take me.

Eyes Wide Open

The next Sunday, I was preaching the assigned lectionary text for the week—and it was John 9, a chapter that is all about seeing. It is about a blind man who is healed by Jesus and is now finally able to see. Since John is the most mystical of the four gospels, it is dense with allegory. The scribes and the Pharisees, the religious leaders who are not able to see, stand in stark contrast to the lowly man who now sees all too well. His sight is a threat to their sense of propriety and religious order. They don't know what to do with him. Their world was more well-ordered when the blind man had his proper place in it.

It's a text not just about physical seeing but about spiritual seeing as well—about the ways that institutional religion often has a vested interest in keeping people blind. It's a story about how the gift of sight is a disruption to the powers that be, the scandal of grace-healed eyes to the powerful. To see from God's perspective is to have the divisions between us and them—the distinctions of class, color, and status—be burned away. Those who have been on the bottom of social structures are able to see themselves differently through the dignity of grace. This also means the same eyes are able to see through the hollow machinations of those in power, able to see that the emperor has no clothes. Religion that is self-serving and self-interested is always threatened by the disruption of new sight. There are political implications to how we see, implications for systems and social structures.

When Jesus comes to town, the blind are able to see. But the converse is also true: Those who think they see the world clearly—those who have too much confidence in their own discernment—are blinded when Jesus comes around. The one who brings sight to the blind brings blindness to those who thought they could see. It's a kind of judgment to be sure, and yet it is great grace. Christ heals the blind, but he cannot heal those who cannot acknowledge their inability to see. Thus for people as deeply religious as I am, grace has to blind us before it can heal us. When the devout religious zealot Saul, an expert in Jewish law, encounters Jesus on the road to Damascus, the light strikes him blind for three days. God wants to make Saul see, but he has to be blinded first. If I was coming to see anything at all, I think that was what was happening to me—I had to go blind if I was ever going to see.

> I had to go blind if I was ever going to see.

When it came time to preach, I did not feel like Moses coming down the mountain to deliver the word of God. I did not feel like delivering a word at all. I only knew that in my broken place, I could speak only of what I was actually seeing, even if my eyes were squinting and I could see only a little. Even if I could see only people who "look like trees," like the blind man touched by Jesus—the man who can't see with clarity until Jesus touches him a second time.[3] The hour was far too late in my fading former life to wax poetic. I could only speak of what I saw.

It was a painful sermon to preach. I told about reading the Irving novel all night the Saturday night before. I told about how I saw how my own lack of suffering had made me relatively aloof to any real suffering in the world—a suffering many marginalized communities know full well—until my own pain and trauma and the pain I felt for hurting others forced me to see. My insides were blistering, and hot tears ran down my face. I was embarrassed for all the things I did not see before, ashamed to acknowledge the lack in my own heart now. I was ashamed I had not owned the people who had always been my people—the hurting, the broken, the marginalized, the outcast. I was ashamed for working so hard to navigate all such matters politically.

In the days and weeks ahead, I finally learned what it meant to lose my life in order to find it. It was a long, slow dying. I was a man who had fallen off the top of a ladder and had still been trying to grab every rung on the way down. I did not yet know that the spiritual life, like Jacob's ladder in the Old Testament, was not just ascent but descent as well. I only knew I did not want to continue to the long fall back to earth.

A Wild Goose Chase

I had been at the Wild Goose Festival campground in Hot Springs, North Carolina, for about ten minutes, not yet having spoken to a single soul, when I heard someone shout my name from across the woods. It was my old friend Steve from my hometown. I was glad to see him, and we exchanged pleasantries. He immediately introduced me to his friend James, who also lives in Charlotte, whose eyes got big when he realized who I was. Apparently, James had just listened to my podcast sermon on learning to see and love people from the underside of things. His best friend had been trying to get James to listen to my podcast forever, but James said he just wasn't interested in listening to sermons—until a few months ago, when his friend insisted he had to listen to this one sermon.

It turned out to be the sermon after I felt like the Holy Spirit came crashing in on me while reading John Irving's *In One Person*. It was the sermon where I talked candidly about feeling like God had gently leveraged my own angst about the state of my own heart and life back onto me as I read the novel, where I recounted the way God spoke to me about keeping certain kinds of stories and certain kinds of people at arm's length. He said it was the most powerful sermon he had ever heard. He said he had distributed it broadly in the LGBTQ community in Charlotte, where James also lived. He proceeded to tell me more of his own story—how he had worked for years behind and in front of the camera in Christian television, most of his career with Pat Robertson's *700 Club*. He told me about the books he published with a major evangelical publisher, trying to walk the straight and narrow as he understood it while struggling violently with his own sexuality. He told the painful story of coming out a few years ago, as chronicled in his last book, *Gay Conversations with God*.

The transparency of my sermon moved him, and he apparently tried to send an email to our office to thank me for it, which I never received. There was so much holiness to that moment that my heart could barely take it in.

We were wrapping up the conversation so I could do my set at the festival—a freestyle sermon with a trance beat behind it—when James somehow casually mentioned the breathing class he led at a yoga studio on Monday nights back in Charlotte. I felt all the blood drain out of my face. I just stood there, stunned, almost too flustered to ask the natural next question I somehow already knew the answer to. "Um, and you were leading this class last Monday night? At Okra in Charlotte? Did you meet someone named Blake Blackman there on Monday?" And of course it was the same guy, and, yes, he had met Blake on Monday and remembered her—as people generally do.

I don't believe every coincidence has to indicate some kind of divine synchronicity. But I strongly believe our God is still moving and speaking today.

After I finished speaking that night, I went back to James's room in a little lodge across the street from the campground and talked with him for several hours. He gave me a copy of his book, and I devoured it through the night before I went to sleep. And in an act that now seems almost ceremonial to me, James, knowing we had forty miles ahead of us before crashing at a hotel, insisted we stay with him for the night. Not only that, but he offered us his room while he slept in a tent. He absolutely would not take no for an answer.

When I had no space, he made space for me.

Guess Who's Coming to Dinner

From that time onward, James became one of my closest friends. Those were not easy times for either of us, and we were given many opportunities to care for one another in the trenches of our lives. One of the great gifts of that season of my life was James always being there to talk, pray, and struggle out loud with me in my own attempt to follow Jesus in my most desolate places. And I think I have been able to be there for him in some of his desolate places too—such grace.

A few months later, I was getting ready to spend Thanksgiving alone. I was going to have a meal with my dad's family the next day, but that day I had no real place to be. Like so much of my life these days, the day was going to be quiet. And I was in a season of learning how to be quiet in a healthy way, to be okay with the fact that the phone didn't ring as much and the inbox wasn't as full.

But when James called and invited me over for Thanksgiving lunch, I have to admit—I was thrilled. Perhaps I was not as okay with the idea of being alone on Thanksgiving as I thought I was.

So I come over to the beautiful house James shares with his friend Greg. Strangely symbolic of my life at the time, I didn't have a dish to bring; I was just there to be fed from their table. I sat around the table with James; Greg; Greg's boyfriend, Kai; their three doting mothers; and a young couple—a man and woman from the UK who are James's friends. (Oh, and the young man is apparently 244th from the throne in England—who knew?) So there you have it—three gay guys; a former Pentecostal pastor trying to get his life together; three sweet, sixty-something Southern moms; and some vague British royalty. What kind of jokes could you make out of all of us walking into a bar?

No longer sitting at the head of Christ's table with the people who decide who is or is not worthy to receive from it, I was the one in need of being loved and accepted. I was given a place at a table that was not my own. I was the wounded one being offered bread and wine I did not deserve. There was no hope or expectation that my new friends would see Jesus in me—only an opportunity to see Jesus animated in the faces of my friends, these icons of grace.

James asked me to pray over the meal—"since we do have a pastor with us today . . ." "Um, former pastor," I said, laughing. Truthfully, I think James and his friends were precisely the people I always longed to be in community with, but I would not have known then how to get to them, or them to me. So if I could be "pastor" enough for the ceremonial prayer for that Thanksgiving meal, I would take it. When we bowed our heads, it took me a full minute to compose myself enough to pray.

As we filled our plates with casseroles, the table was filling up with stories. We talked about our brokenness, and we talked about our joy. There had never been a place, a moment, or a meal I had been more thankful for than that place, that moment, that meal. The Thanksgiving I had most dreaded was the most beautiful one I had ever had. I felt the same tremble in my lips I get when I take the chalice each Sunday while kneeling to receive Communion.

The Blasphemous Posture
of Looking Down

How much of my life have I actually spent in hours of conversations about who is in and who is out of God's kingdom? Conversations where I was articulate, even compassionate, even honest. But now I see that all academic conversations, all theoretical discussions, are in their own way untruthful, no matter how honest you try to be. Even when you are well armed with Bible verses, commentaries, and research papers, how truthful can any conversation be when you are sitting at the head of the table? That was the life I had before I experienced profound brokenness, suffering, and shame—the life lived from the shallows and not from the depths.

I don't claim—any more now than I ever did—to have all the answers to complex questions of faith and life, and I would not proffer any here. More than enough ink has been spilled in service of these issues, from all angles and positions. What I care about is perspective, which unlocks the door to any authentic wisdom. My simple appeal is not to trust your own, especially when you're judging the world from on top of it. I wonder if we ever know much of anything about anybody until we are on our backs and in the position of needing God and the image of God in others.

Conservatives, liberals, and everyone in between can offer all kinds of positions on life and the world and the other, and the bottom line is that if you speak their insider language, you can be part of their in crowd and get the insider benefits.

The trouble is that God doesn't exist in idea; God doesn't exist in theory—and people don't exist in idea or theory either. God is only found in dirt-floor reality. God is only found in the vulnerability of a manger with the stench of manure, teaching us how to be human by relying on other humans. God is only found on the cross, with his insides exposed, leaking out to the world for the sake of its healing.

When we're too proud to be on our backs—in a manger or on a cross—we can be as honest as we know how to be, but the world we see is still founded on lies. When we can't see life from the underside, we can't see the people around us for who they really are, nor can we see the world for what it truly is. It is blasphemy to take the posture of the high place from which we look down at everyone else, at the world we see only as below us. It is a posture that the God who made the world is far too humble to take himself.

No, the truth about God, ourselves, and the world can only be truly seen from the underside. That is where Jesus works his miracles.

> When we can't see life from the underside, we can't see the people around us for who they really are, nor can we see the world for what it truly is.

Chapter Nine

The City beneath the Sea

He felt the full warmth of that pleasure from which the proud shut themselves out; the pleasure which not only goes with humiliation, but which almost is humiliation. Men who have escaped death by a hair have it . . . and men whose sins are forgiven them. Everything his eye fell on it feasted on, not aesthetically, but with a plain, jolly appetite as of a boy eating buns . . . He was, perhaps, the happiest of all the children of men. For in that unendurable instant when he hung, half slipping, to the ball of St. Paul's, the whole universe had been destroyed and re-created.

G. K. Chesterton

There is an undeniable power that comes from living out of the depths, out of an ancient current that is bigger and deeper than you are. There is a deeper capacity for pain when you live from your soul. Ironically enough, the clang of your own life hitting the ground is the big bang wherein all new life begins. The first discovery of the shipwreck is that we have a higher capacity for pain than we ever could have imagined before we lost, before we failed, or before we suffered. You don't know the depth of your soul until whole chunks of you are falling into the bottom of it. The pain, initially, is disorienting—the sound of a thousand car bombs going off all around you. You cannot think, cannot move, cannot breathe. For a while, the acute awareness of loss is the only reality that you know. Every sensory part of you throbs, aches, bleeds, until it feels like there are no more tears to cry or blood to spill.

The surprise on the other side of the shipwreck is that, while your capacity for pain proved to be far beyond your wildest reckoning, now you have a capacity to feel everything deeper. You are capable of a depth of empathy and compassion that would have been unthinkable before. When you fully embrace the pain of your journey, fully own the darkness of your own story all the way down, you are on the road to wholeness, even while you're still in pieces. The reality is, the version of the self that existed before the pain was the one that was fractured and fragmented. Your life, on the surface of things, had the appearance of wholeness, but too many things inside you were detached.

As you slowly start to become whole—no matter how broken you feel—there is an essential unity now, a mysterious integration that is happening in the depths. This is the territory where body, mind, and spirit begin to regain their native unity; where the inner and outer life are coming into harmony; the intersection where the spiritual and material worlds slowly weave into one. You are humble enough to know now that you are no angel, no matter who praises you. You are wise enough to know now that you are no devil, no matter who damns you. You are a real boy or a real girl, a real-life human being—capable of great love and deep failure, strength and imperfection, beauty and flaws. You are nothing more and nothing less, and the shipwreck has a way of making peace with all of these divergent parts of yourself. You have no misplaced confidence in yourself, nor are you subject to self-loathing any longer. You are human in the holiest and most broken sense of the word, in all the ways that God became and said you could become. You are learning to live in the mystery of incarnation, for the words of life and peace you carried like seeds now grow into skin and flesh and blood. You are learning to live in imitation of the triune God— Father, Son, and Holy Spirit—as a whole, gathered, unified self.

> You are learning to live in imitation of the triune God— Father, Son, and Holy Spirit—as a whole, gathered, unified self.

The first steps in this new skin are wobbly at best. On the other side of the shipwreck, you feel like you have to learn to walk again, to talk again, to breathe again. Out of the wreckage, something green and hopeful is starting to emerge; the smell of a newborn baby's head. And from this newfound capacity for pain, for sorrow, for torment, for agony, for endless waves of grief, comes the biggest surprise of them all—your newfound capacity for joy. You did not know you could suffer so intensely. Neither did you know you could experience joy this intensely. How could you have known that one day you'd have a meal again where every taste bud would explode with sensation? How could you have known that from this ferocious capacity for hurt could come such an intensity of loving?

How could you have ever known you could be this alive, until you died?

The Island of Misfit Broken Toys

For all the merits of a life of safety, security, and certitude, life before the shipwreck is so often compartmentalized. It seems we don't often know how to live as a unified, integrated self until the world we knew is underwater, and the powerful river that ran beneath us floods our surface. The heartbreak and sheer grief of what we lost in the water can threaten to swallow us up entirely. Even if we make it to shore, like Paul and his companions floating on pieces of the ship did, the journey took far too much out of us for us to be celebrating any arrival too much—the journey itself has been far too humbling.

And yet what I hear repeatedly from people who survive a shipwreck of any sort is that the life they live on the other side is simpler, cleaner, more coherent, more focused. We are learning to live after the model of the Trinity, of the God who is three-in-one, instead of dividing ourselves. We are no longer spinning the information or maintaining the ego. The life we live is becoming more and more the life we have chosen, whole and authentic—however unspectacular it might seem. The old distinctions of us and them, sacred and secular, body and spirit, are washed away in the flood's purifying waters. For the first time for many of us, life on the other side of the shipwreck holds the promise of an integrated life—a life that incorporates night and not just day, darkness and not just light, body and not just mind. It's a life that incorporates dark matter honestly, a life where all of you and your story is welcomed rather than shunned—even and perhaps especially the unsightly parts of you.

In my own shipwreck season, learning how to depend on others—how to need and ask for help—one of the most crucial legs of the journey was the month I spent in New Orleans with my friends Tim and Barbara Gilbert. They opened their home to me when my heart was still in tatters, living that ghost life, yet without closure to much of anything. Through the time I spent with them, both then and many times since, New Orleans has become a kind of spiritual home for me, the place where I most find myself. I think that's largely due to the ways that NOLA eradicates the false division of sacred and secular, as well as the place it has in my personal history. When I went back to New Orleans in 2014, it was the first time I had been there since I was a child—and the way I experienced it this time changed everything.

While I stayed with the Gilberts, I felt like I was slowly being nursed back to health. They took me to New Orleans's unbelievably diverse restaurants, to see Pelicans games, to see a Dave Chappelle stand-up show in a theater on Canal Street. They made me feel safe to let my soul out in a city that demands you live no other way. I would go to St. Louis Cathedral in the mornings to pray, and then to the Carousel Bar at the Hotel Monteleone (where literature luminaries from Hemingway to Faulkner to Eudora Welty famously stayed) to write all afternoon. Somewhere at the intersections of these two places, my life was being patched back together.

What better place to learn there is life on the other side of the shipwreck than in the city that found new life after the flood? The city beneath the sea has been under water, should be under water—and yet it keeps finding a way to survive, keeps finding a way to make music, from the underside. The levees broke, but the spirit of the city could not be broken. I needed New Orleans to tell me her secrets. One afternoon, I wrote a little love song to New Orleans, which for me now stands as the power of the shipwreck to thrust you, with or without your consent, into an integrated life. No better place to learn such things than the city beneath the sea.

⁓

I remember the first time I came to New Orleans in the distant way one remembers some near-forgotten dream. I remember her like a ghost, like a shadow. I remember the feel of her in my body more than any particular image of her in my head. I was fourteen years old, and the occasion, ironically enough, was the biannual meeting of our conservative Pentecostal denomination. Even now it's hard to imagine the people who populated my childhood walking those dreamy, steamy streets.

The air felt full of sex and salt water. Church of God preachers in their suits and ties and women in their long

Sunday dresses were walking down Bourbon Street on their way to worship at the Superdome. Pentecostals, historically, are misfit people, products of the kind of sweaty spirituality that could only be given birth on the wrong side of the railroad tracks. But I would have never known how to pair the bodily, ecstatic worship of the Pentecostals with the kind of sensuous delight offered on Bourbon Street. The churches I grew up in, like New Orleans, had a penchant for colorful characters that seemed to walk out of a Flannery O'Connor short story—the fluid, free-flowing improvisation of jazz music, loud clothes, and a carnival atmosphere. But the sacred and the secular were not on speaking terms; they were as distant as Jerry Lee Lewis from his infamous cousin, Jimmy Swaggart.

I still remember watching the pack of preachers in front of me walk past a stand selling novelty ties made to look like penises (which instinctively seems like it should read "peni"). There was a store on the left where the mannequins were decked out in an assortment of vinyl, leather, and lace. Walking past the seedy club across the street that advertised seedy performances, I felt the sea in me stir. It was foreign and exciting. And terrifying. I cut my eyes away quickly to the dirty concrete beneath my feet, scared to death by this strange city and my own longing. I walked the French Quarter as a stranger, just a pilgrim passing through on my way to the Superdome, where the saints were marching in awkwardly—and hopefully one day to heaven. I walked the street as I walked the world so much of my life—as a bystander, a spectator, and not as a citizen of the parade.

Looking back, I never really learned how to be at home in either world, because I never learned how to be at home in my own skin. I longed for the ecstasy around me in the tent revival every bit as much as I longed for the ecstasy around me on Bourbon Street, but I lived too much in my head to get down into my soul and my body. I was stuck in my mind and on the surface of things. In both places, I was too afraid and too self-conscious to get lost in the music. I believed in all of the Pentecostal business. I wanted the jazz in me, the dance in me, the life in me—the life Jesus talked about when he said of a believer, "Out of his belly shall flow rivers of living water."[1] God have mercy, I wanted the life that could only be lived from my belly. Then and now, I want to crackle; I want to howl; I want to rumble. I want to talk in tongues.

Twenty-two years later, I walk down Bourbon Street on a clear December morning. I taste the boozy, swampy smell in the back of my throat. The daylight settles in the French Quarter like a hangover—it feels less like today than the morning after. The city is coming awake like a slow storm rising. There's a jazz band setting up on the sidewalk just ahead, and from a distance, I hear a trombone playing outside the St. Louis Cathedral. A man in a suit smoking a slim cigarette approaches when I walk past the strip club. "Come on in," he says. "We've got cold beers and warm nipples inside!"

I cut up St. Peter Street to get to the cathedral. There are folding tables set up just outside, offering palm readings from voodoo spirit guides. As I step through the heavy doors, the smell of sex gives way to Spirit, and I effortlessly slip into the wonder. I walk to the third row on the right, feeling my soul already finding sanctuary in the reverence. Kneeling, I begin to pray through my beads, taking slow, deep breaths between the psalm I'm meditating on. St. Louis Cathedral is in the middle of the carnival, the way God always is.

Melting into the presence, awareness creeps through my very bones, and I know God is not only in this place, but in all the places I walked past to get here. God in the St. Charles streetcar I rode in on, in the old black man in the gold and black Saints toboggan cap sitting beside me; God in the white man with beady eyes in the polyester suit, summoning tourists into the cathedral with no windows— those who are on their own search for transcendence. God in the woman with the dreads reading tarot cards just outside the entrance to the church; God in the dazzling art that climbs all the way onto the roof of the cathedral. In the decadence and in the piety, Love itself is sustaining us, making us exist. "In him we live and move and have our being," the apostle Paul wrote, assuring us we are always in the presence of the one who is not far from each of us.[2] In the breathing, my soul knows again there is nowhere God is not. Pressing softly into the divine, all the dualisms are dissolved. There is no us and them, no sacred and profane. There is the Love that exists at the center of things, and us, like sheep, who stumble into or out of awareness of the one who calls us into existence.

What better place to learn this than the city beneath the sea? New Orleans knows that sex and spirituality, voodoo and Catholicism, are two sides of the same mystery. She knows that these little humans all want to get lost more than get found, to drift into a mystery larger than themselves. "The young man who rings the bell at the brothel is unconsciously looking for God," Bruce Marshall wrote. She knows that the ordered world is an illusion, so the things we keep under the surface she puts out on the street. She knows that whatever cathedrals we wander into to pay homage, whether the gods on the wall are Jack Daniels or Jesus

> Whatever cathedrals we wander into to pay homage, whether the gods on the wall are Jack Daniels or Jesus Christ, we are all looking to let go.

Christ, we are all looking to let go. We're all looking to lose ourselves—into the night and into the wonder. Deep down, we all want to be all in, somewhere—anywhere—as long as we are in over our heads.

The first time I came to New Orleans, everything in my world was sharply divided. The dualisms of head and heart, body and spirit, light and dark, good guys and bad guys, were already bone-deep. My world was divided into us and them. That's the floor beneath us when we are walking above sea level. The world cannot change until we fall into the ocean, or the rain comes and floods us right where we are. New Orleans, a saucer twenty feet below sea level, wears these secrets like a scar. She knows that in reality, a flood is always around the corner; we just didn't know it until we had one of our own. But the saints and sinners go marching in here without fear. She knows in her bones, after all, that there is life after the flood. The nightmare of Katrina had its way with the city of dreams, and the levees broke. The waters were merciless, and the losses unfathomable. But she dances still, because she knows the secret of death and resurrection. She knows that crisis brings all her misfits together. She knows that after the flood, you make new life and make love the same way she has always made music—by trusting the people around you enough to improvise. She knows there is life on the long side of dying.

In the old New Orleans tradition, even a funeral is followed by a parade. The first line of participants is the friends and family escorting the casket. The second line is comprised of the crowd, any passersby who want to join the processional. She is not afraid of death, because she knows even dying is an invitation to a deeper, more authentic way of living, an invitation to join the parade.

When I came back to New Orleans, I came back after my own flood. The life that felt so safe, comfortable, and familiar was under the sea, and everything I once loved was under water. I had lost heart, lost hope, and lost myself in the depths. In other words, I was finally ready to understand the city beneath the sea. It's no wonder, then, sitting in that open-air café, watching the people outside St. Louis Cathedral, there was no more us and them. I could be kin with the Asian tourists and the grizzly, bearded palm reader, and the children on the field trip—happier with each other than impressed by the austere beauty of St. Louis Cathedral. I felt like I belonged on New Orleans' island of drunken, misfit toys. Instead of judging her, I came longing for this city of second chances to make room for me around her table too. Nobody's past is counted against them here. New Orleans doesn't smell like just sex and salt water to me anymore.

She smells like the gospel.

Leaving Home

Charlotte, North Carolina, was the only home I had ever known in my thirty-seven years. For as much as I may have griped from time to time about the "Christ-haunted land-scape" of the American South, it was the soil of me, where all my songs and stories grew roots in me. Like the Kings of Leon song, somewhere deep down, I was a pretty big proponent of "just drink the water where you came from."

It was there that I had done all of my living, and all of my falling in love. It was the home of the Church of God campground where I had my first kiss and my first taste of the Holy Ghost. It was where my grandfather turned in his badge and gun as a Charlotte-Mecklenburg police officer and said God called him to preach. It was there that I went to this little, private Christian school in the fifth grade, where one day after school I was jumping back and forth over a small brick wall in the courtyard—tripping and gashing open my shin, where I have a permanent scar to this day. It was that same property that Renovatus Church inherited more than twenty years later, where I'd fall again and spill infinitely more blood on the ground. By the time you've done that much living and that much dying, all on the same ground, your heart has no other place to call home.

But that brings me back to the story I told in chapter 1,

about being in the bar where the ghost of the pastor of Renovatus accosted, and where I started to finally accept that the life I had—I was no longer really living. I had become, if not comfortable, quite settled into the life of a ghost flickering on the walls of my hometown, feeling myself of no substance, as if I was somehow vanishing before my eyes and the eyes of my handful of friends and family. On the other side of the church, I still loved my city and the people in it as much as I did when I got started. I had always loved those people and never really had any dream beyond being a pastor in the place I grew up. There was still some weight on my sense of call there, even if there was precious little substance left in my bones. I didn't have many friends or exactly a real job anymore. But even ghosts like familiar places to haunt.

In many ways, I guess I was running. Not ultimately from any of the old places, not from any of the people I loved (though I did that too), but from myself. The trouble with this, of course, is that the only person you can't outrun is yourself. Still, it felt like I had to find a way to start over somewhere else if I was going to find a way to be new. I was going to have to follow the wind.

It seemed to be blowing to the oddest of places—to Tulsa, Oklahoma, where my friend Ed Gungor served as pastor of a church called Sanctuary. I loved Ed and his church, but I couldn't imagine life away from the only home I had known for my thirty-seven years. And yet, I knew Sanctuary was the kind of community I could invest in, the kind of community that works hard at becoming whole together. And I felt God in the wind, calling me to become part of it.

Exhausted, heartbroken, but with a little fire left in my bones—just enough, I hoped—I took off for Oklahoma and left my whole life behind. I hoped that in this, I was finally losing my life to find it. But God knows, I had never felt more lost or more alone. The void was deep black and seemed to run all the way through me. The chaos was thick with nothingness. And yet, even as I sat in the abyss of my former life gone dark, I felt the stirrings of the Spirit, brooding overhead, despite myself.

The wind was blowing over me, not a violent rushing wind now, but a wind nonetheless. And finally, I had no strength left to fight it.

The Sound of Being Born

I was afraid Tulsa would feel like exile, so foreign to the only life I formerly knew. But instead the town itself became synonymous with the name of the church there—a sanctuary.

I had been in Tulsa for a little more than a month about the time U2's "Songs of Innocence and Experience" tour was coming to an end. I had not missed a North American U2 tour in twenty years and was seized with the impulse that I could not bear to miss one now. A lifelong fan who had been to fifteen shows, I actually wasn't sure I was ready for the emotion I knew would be waiting at the door of the arena if I showed up then. But for all that had changed and was still changing, the wide-open spaces of U2's music had always felt to me like home. So just days before the show,

I splurged to make it all happen—a last-minute flight to New York City to the next-to-the-last show of the tour in Madison Square Garden.

I was in the city for less than twenty-four hours. I had been there a number of times before, but never like this—on the other side of a shipwreck, on these unsteady new feet, as a stranger to my new life. It was alien, and it was magical. Down on the floor, a few feet from the stage, letting all of me out into the wideness of sound, I sang out my old innocence and sang into my own songs of experience, going from the garden into the depths of hell and came back round again. I already had quite a soul history with the song "Beautiful Day," a tune about the life that begins with the sky falling. But I had never had the sky fall like this before. I had never lost so much. And thus, I had never known such skin-bursting new life—a thing that came out of my chest cavity during that show as I sang along with Bono at the top of my lungs: "What you don't have you don't need it now." God, yes.

During the song "City of Blinding Lights," while Bono was singing, "Blessing's not just for the ones who kneel, luckily," I am weeping. Because I know that whether or not I feel I have a proper claim on these new gifts, God is the one who is giving them. And in the same way that the shipwreck taught me to open my hands and open my life and let the waves have their way with me; now I had to give myself over to waves of blessing sweeping over me just as much. Again here comes the Spirit, sweeping over the face of the waters—like she always does.

Throughout the tour, the band had been playing a cover

of Paul Simon's beautiful "Mother and Child Reunion" during the encore: It's a song that moves me deeply—a song Simon wrote after his dog died in 1971—and how I missed my sweet little dog back in North Carolina. How I missed everything. It's a song about not giving "false hope," and about how unrealistic it is in grief to follow the counsel of the Beatles a few years before and just "let it be." And yet there is this message embedded too: There is still a reunion possible somewhere on the other side, "only a motion away." That maybe there is a space just beyond this one where all the things we can't make right on this side of the veil will be made right still. That there is a reunion on the other side of us where we can be reunited with all those we feel estranged from now—in a kingdom big enough for all of them, with new hearts big enough to love and embrace them all. And their hearts will be large enough too, in this spaciousness of grace, to embrace us back, past all of our sins against them.

Since it was New York City and the end of the tour, there was Paul Simon, just in front of the stage. The seventy-three-year-old songwriter got up on stage to join U2, while Bono bowed and sang it through with the band behind him. I heard myself pray out loud, "My God." I felt a reunion in my own soul with my own God, with my own life. I was not yet at home in the world—and in some ways may never be . . . until the day. But at least I was at home inside my own skin again and in my weary bones.

If there was still some ambiguity about whether or not the hoped-for reunion can or will be realized, U2's guitarist The Edge answered the question, chiming out the opening chords to the band's most soulish anthem, "Where the Streets Have No Name." If that is not what being born again sounds like, what is?

I still don't know how to make soul music. But God knows I had finally found my own shout.

The Doors of the Sea

I have written about shipwreck and about surviving the sea. Sometimes that is all we can do. Yet Christian hope is ultimately not that the sea can be survived but that the sea will one day be eliminated—in the time when time as we know it is no more. Stranded on the island of Patmos, John wrote an apocalypse. It was a vision born out of great pain, in the way most visions are. Perhaps he wrote these words while looking out at the sea:

> Then I saw a new heaven and a new earth; for the first heaven and the first earth had passed away, and the sea was no more. And I saw the holy city, the new Jerusalem, coming down out of heaven from God, prepared as a bride adorned for her husband. And I heard a loud voice from the throne saying,
>
> > "See, the home of God is among mortals.
> > He will dwell with them;
> > they will be his peoples,
> > and God himself will be with them;
> > he will wipe every tear from their eyes.

Death will be no more;

mourning and crying and pain will be no more,

for the first things have passed away."[3]

With this, the story of the New Testament comes to an end, as the holy city comes down. Death and sorrow are abolished, and God wipes away all tears—all things are made new. But the pronouncement of the world that can and must yet come is first heralded by a stark, stunning announcement of what will be absent in the restoration of all things: "The sea was no more." Five simple words that say everything.

The sea, which from the beginning represented chaos, the tumultuous unknowing, the place where all the monsters come from in the book of Daniel, the home of Leviathan and billions of buried children, buried treasures, and buried dreams—will be no more. The world that is coming will not be marked by ambiguity, angst, and chaos. Instead, the Spirit who brooded over the waters from the beginning brings the creation project to its final end—where the seeds of the dark void finally give way to endless flowers. Because in the death of Jesus of Nazareth death itself died, all pain will be finally swallowed up by resurrection. The flames of the Spirit's fire will finally transfigure the world from its unending travail into something altogether new—with an explosion of love and color and great laughter. The world birthed by the God of infinite hope already reverberates as beauty crackles through it like sacred electricity. So then she must yet yield to a final spasm into new life—new and new and new and new, waves of newness for humans and plants and animals and trees, as the Spirit comes again for one more sweep over the remaining chaos. This God, according to Revelation, has bottled up the tears of the saints, held and collected all of our collective heartbreak, storing them for the day they are mingled with the river of life. The sea with all of its violence will be forever tamed by the terrible tenderness of the Lamb, who overcomes the powers of death by his own sacrifice.

What can we say about this world where the lamb and the lion lay side by side, the child plays over the den of the adder, and all created things rest in the safety of God's holy mountain? How can we fathom a world in which Leviathan, the dread of a thousand grizzled sailors, is a harmless pet pulled gently around by the hook in his nose? There is no distinction anymore between heaven and earth, or light and dark, or us and them—everything melts at last into good.

The God who will do this is not just loving but is Love himself. A being with the ferocity of all light in the cosmos is not in need of my defending, but I want to put in a final word for this God revealed in Jesus anyway, over and against all our ways of speaking that impugn the name of God. This God, contrary to popular opinion in some circles, is the one who tames the sea, not the one who stirs its monsters into action. This God does not assault people with the elements to teach them moral lessons. This God does not script all of our sorrows as part of some cosmic plan. The death and resurrection of Jesus have already neutered the power of death and unceremoniously removed its sting. Death, in the end, is not an ally God cooperates with to bring about his good purposes for the world, but an enemy he will overthrow.

Along with all the pain and violence of the world, Love will finally burn away the damnable doctrines of demons that turn the Savior of the world into the kind of monster he came to save us from—that say there are some people he destines for destruction, that he gets some abstract kind of glory out of tragic car wrecks, that he engineers praise out of mothers with cancer and babies with AIDS. This God is not some rogue FBI agent on a TV show who uses instruments of torture to bring about some greater good in the world. This is the God who let himself be tortured on our behalf and exposed the weakness of all instruments of terror and death by the power of his own unfailing love. We know what this God is like because we know this God is like Jesus.

Don't let anybody ever tell you lies, however well-intentioned they may be, about this good God. Don't let anybody ever tell you that the one who cherishes and bottles your tears has ever been the author of your pain. Don't let anybody ever tell you that he allies with death when it's the only thing he came to overthrow. As long as you believe in a god like that, you cannot truly believe in a benevolent God, no matter how loving you try to convince yourself he is. As long as you believe in a god like that, you are not yet living in a benevolent universe, but in a realm in which death and darkness still reign.

I have written broadly about shipwreck, including the ones of our own making—of my own making, in particular. But I am especially sensitive here to those who have endured some kind of trauma that seemed to fall from the sky itself and who were comforted by the friends of Job, calling themselves the friends of Jesus. You may have been given some kind of platitude about how it was all part of God's plan or how something good is going to come out of this—or been given some kind of an explanation for why it happened the way it did. The truth about the sea and the chaos is that there are no explanations. The error of Job's friends was not just that their explanations for his suffering were wrong, but that they tried to give a rational explanation to human suffering at all. The only hope we can offer is the kind of ultimate hope given in the book of Revelation: The wounds that cannot and will not be made right in this life will be made right in the world to come—that grand and final reunion, of mother and child.

In the book of Job, God asks Job:

> "Or who shut in the sea with doors
>   when it burst out from the womb?—
> when I made the clouds its garment,
>   and thick darkness its swaddling band,
> and prescribed bounds for it,
>   and set bars and doors,
> and said, 'Thus far shall you come, and no farther,
>   and here shall your proud waves be stopped'?"[4]

God is the one who shut the sea with doors from the beginning so all of creation would not be entirely consumed by the chaos. God was the one who kept the world from being utterly overwhelmed by violence from the absolute rule of the monsters that lie in the sea. But in the end, God will not shut the doors to the sea merely to draw a boundary as he did in the beginning—but he will eliminate it entirely. I suspect there will yet be oceans to sail in the world to come, and a hundred million miles of white sands along the shore. But the sea, with its unending depths of terror and ambiguity, its threat of shipwreck, simply has no place in the world that is coming.

> God has exactly one plan—and it is to bring the reign of heaven into the depths of the earth, eliminating the sea of our shipwrecks once and for all.

Until then, may we not offer false hope to those who suffer. Let us not offer words of tepid comfort either—platitudes about a God who "has a plan," and a plan that demands our suffering. I believe God has exactly one plan—and it is to bring the reign of heaven into the depths of the earth, eliminating the sea of our shipwrecks once and for all.

In the words of David Bentley Hart:

> As for comfort, when we seek it, I can imagine none greater than the happy knowledge that when I see the death of a child, I do not see the face of God but the face of his enemy . . . it is a faith that set us free from optimism long ago and taught us hope instead. Now we are able to rejoice that we are saved not through the immanent mechanisms of history and nature, but by grace; that God will not unite all of history's many strands in one great synthesis, but will judge much of history false and damnable; that he will not simply

reveal the sublime logic of fallen nature, but will strike off the fetters in which creation languishes; and that, rather than showing us how the tears of a small girl suffering in the dark were necessary for the building of the Kingdom, he will instead raise her up and wipe away all tears from her eyes—and there shall be no more death, nor sorrow, nor crying, nor any more pain, for the former things will have passed away, and he that sits upon the throne will say, "Behold, I make all things new."[5]

Please Don't Drown Today

I hope something of what I've learned through my own shipwreck can help you survive your own. I'd love it if words written from my own pain help somehow to assuage your own. And yet I know all too well there is a pain so dark and so deep that words cannot survive in the depths of it. I do not presume I can write anything capable of making it all better. But at the very least, I hope these words may yet be enough to keep the light on in you for a little while longer. I am in no place, of course, to tell you what to do, much less to ask anything of you while you sort out the remains of your own once-sturdy ship. But I must ask one thing, because if you cannot do this, the rest will not matter. And whether my own prayers make it above the swirl of the winds around me, I hurl them into the clouds for you, even as I write now, so that this plea carries the smell of prayer, my seawater incense.

Please do not give up. You can think about it again tomorrow if you have to, but please not today. Please do not let yourself drown. Please do not let the merciless tides tread over your precious head. There is so much life for you. I know, because I've found it. And dear God, I want the same for you.

I may not know your precise coordinates on the map, not exactly. But I know well the sand beneath you, and I know the dreams that have been dashed against those rocks, as well as I know my own. So I also know that when the days and nights stretch into forever, despair whispers in the clouds to you like a siren. And the voice whistles through the holes in you that your best days are behind, and that there are no reasons left for you to try. I know, your reasons floated out with the tide, along with almost everything else you had on board. I know despair serenades you, and that her voice is even soft. I know your battered soul is the only treasure you have left to carry, and why it's so tempting now to let go of it too—to lie down in the water as your bed, and let the waves wash over you slow until the tide takes you into the forever night.

You may not feel like you have any reasons left to resist her. But at the very least, your existence alone is a reason for the rest of us not to lose heart. Your life is a sign and a sacrament for someone, a light in someone else's darkness. I don't know how I know this, but I know this. And if it is hard to imagine another reason to stay on this ghost town shore for one more day, I will ask you selfishly to stay alive tonight—for me. I will ask you as the ambassador of a whole tribe of shipwrecked souls you do not yet know, in lands near and far you cannot yet see, for whom also your life will yet be great grace. As much as you may have felt like you lost yourself, your presence in this world is enough for somebody else to feel found.

It is not that I think death is a thing for you to fear. There will be many times and many ways you will have to let go into the night, and many currents you can trust to lead you to people and places you need to know. I am not even telling you to hang on to your life. I am telling you there's a light inside you that does need to be held on to, a flame that the harsh elements might snuff out if you let them.

You will one day lose your life, as we all will. But in the living and the dying and all that happens in between, you don't have to lose your fire. And if you listen to the shadows that tell you to despair of life, even if some function of duty or obligation propels you to keep on living, the world will miss the flame that burns in you. When there is so much cold and there is so much night, you are so much more heat and light than you know.

I have told you what little I know about surrender—about letting go, and the kind of life that can come on the other side of laying down your life eventually. But it won't be the same thing as giving up, and it won't be the same thing as letting the light in you go out.

Your soul is warm and full of light, however weathered. Don't let it go out, don't let it float away. All you have to do is stay a little longer here in this desolate in-between space.

All you have to do is stay here in the chaos and be present to it, even to its deep blackness. Stay here, even if it means attending to your pain, and stay alert.

Please, just don't lose heart. Don't give up the ghost.

Just stay here for a little while longer.

This is not all there is. There is another wind, coming in slow on the wings of the morning, to hover over your still-flickering light to make you into fire again.

Acknowledgments

This book has felt like such a fragile, vulnerable, but hard-edged thing, difficult to write and yet impossible not to. Given its sensitive nature, it has been especially wonderful to feel such complete support from my delightful team at Zondervan. I am particularly thankful for my brilliant editor, Stephanie Smith, for engaging this project with so much heart. I'm grateful for my agent Don Jacobson, for all the ways he has believed in and championed this project.

I've written a lot about recognizing frailty, learning to be contingent and dependent, and learning to put real weight on people you love and who you know love you. It has been especially humbling to have such a gracious community to lift me when I needed lifting the most—people who have kept me afloat. There is no way I'd have survived the shipwreck long enough to write about it without them. So I offer my heartfelt thanks to my beautiful parents, Ron and Lynda Martin, for never letting go (and helping me believe in a God who wouldn't let go either); my community at Sanctuary Church in Tulsa, Oklahoma, for teaching me how to walk again—especially Ed Gungor, Brent and Janis Sharpe, Cody Jefferson, Shelby Swanson, Paul Paino, and Ashley Hinden; my adopted family, Tim and Barbara Gilbert, for opening their hearts and their home in New Orleans to me; my remarkable friends, new and old, who have seen me through the night—Chris Green, Aaron and Shauna Niequist, Steven Furtick, Ben and Noelle Kilgore, Jarrod McKenna, Mark and Danielle Aarstad, Randall Worley, William Matthews, Brian Zahnd, and James Alexander Langteaux; and my spiritual grandmother, Sister Margaret Gaines, for teaching me everything I need to know about Jesus just by being who she is.

Notes

Chapter One: Losing Your Ship without Losing Your Soul

1. Matthew 28.10.
2. Luke 10.18, NIV.
3. Luke 22.31–32.
4. Acts 27.34.

Chapter Two: How Not to Survive a Shipwreck

1. John 21.18, NIV.
2. G. K. Chesterton, *The Illustrated London News 1908–10*, in The Collected Works of G. K. Chesterton, vol. 28 (San Francisco: Ignatius, 1987), 17.
3. Matthew 23.15.
4. Thomas Merton, *Conjectures of a Guilty Bystander* (Garden City, N.Y.: Doubleday, 1966), 153–55.
5. 1 Corinthians 1.18.
6. Barbara Brown Taylor, *Leaving Church* (New York: HarperCollins, 2006), 119–20.

Chapter Three: Hold On, Let Go

1. Acts 27.20.
2. John 20.17, my paraphrase.

3. Acts 17.28.
4. Psalm 139.7–12.
5. Thomas Merton, *Love and Living* (New York: Farrar, Straus Giroux, 1979), 11–12.

Chapter Four: Eating, Breathing, Sleeping

1. Acts 27.33–38, NIV.
2. Matthew 6.11.
3. Acts 17.28.
4. Acts 17.28.
5. Psalm 139.8–10, NIV.
6. Frederick Buechner, *Whistling in the Dark: A Doubter's Dictionary* (San Francisco: HarperCollins, 1993), 114.
7. Frederick Buechner, *The Alphabet of Grace* (San Francisco: HarperCollins, 1970), 25.

Chapter Five: God Loves Monsters

1. See Job 1.6.
2. Job 16.3.
3. René Girard, *Job: The Victim of His People* (Redwood City, Calif.: Stanford University Press, 1987).
4. Luke 23.34.
5. Romans 5.8.
6. Job 7.11–12.
7. Job 9.16–19.
8. From the Voice translation of Job 9.13.
9. Job 26.12–13.
10. Job 41.1–2, 8–11.
11. Job 41.13.
12. Job 41.19.
13. Job 41.18, 21, 26–27.
14. Job 41.25–26, 31–34.

15. Job 41.9–11, as paraphrased by Timothy K. Beal, *Religion and Its Monsters* (New York: Routledge, 2002), 51.
16. Genesis 1.21.
17. Beal, *Religion and Its Monsters*, 55.
18. Psalm 139.12.
19. 1 John 1.7.
20. 1 John 1.8, NIV.
21. Matthew 5.45, ESV.
22. Gustavo J. Gutiérrez, *On Job: God-Talk and the Suffering of the Innocent* (Maryknoll, N.Y.: Orbis, 1987), 88–89.
23. Frederick Buechner, *Wishful Thinking* (New York: Harper and Row, 1973), 99.
24. James Joyce, "The Dead," in *Dubliners* (New York: Viking, 1967), 67.

Chapter Six: Choose Your Own Adventure

1. Matthew 23.15.
2. 1 John 4.18.
3. Margaret Wise Brown, *The Runaway Bunny* (New York: Harper and Row, 1942), 1.
4. Elizabeth Lesser, *Broken Open: How Difficult Times Can Help Us Grow* (New York: Random House, 2004), 174.
5. Psalm 139.9–10.
6. Lesser, *Broken Open*, 175.
7. Rollo May, *Man's Search for Himself* (New York: Norton, 2009), 125.
8. Ibid., 126.
9. Matthew 23.15.
10. May, *Man's Search for Himself*, 148.
11. Ibid., 177.
12. Romans 6.23.
13. Luke 15.11–32.
14. 1 Corinthians 13.12, KJV.
15. 1 Corinthians 13.11.

16. Acts 17.28.
17. Parker J. Palmer, *Let Your Life Speak* (San Francisco: Jossey-Bass, 1999), 54.
18. Bruce Marshall, *The World, the Flesh and Father Smith* (Boston: Houghton Mifflin, 1945), 108.
19. 1 Corinthians 3.9, ESV.
20. Augustine, "Sermon on 1 John 4.4–12."

Chapter Seven: Don't Fight the Wind

1. Acts 2.2.
2. Genesis 1.1–2, emphasis added.
3. James Joyce, *Finnegan's Wake* (New York: Penguin, 1999), 118.21–23.
4. Hebrews 12.26–29.
5. Exodus 19.
6. Matthew 16.17.

Chapter Eight: Starting to See

1. Isaiah 53.3, ESV.
2. John 21.18, NIV.
3. Mark 8.24–25.

Chapter Nine: The City beneath the Sea

1. John 7.38, KJV.
2. Acts 17.27–28.
3. Revelation 21.1–5.
4. Job 38.8–11.
5. David Bentley Hart, *The Doors of the Sea* (Grand Rapids: Eerdmans, 2011), 103–4.